From
SCHOOLBOY
to
SOLDIER

EDWARD STANLEY ABBOT
OCTOBER 22, 1841–JULY 8, 1863

From
SCHOOLBOY
to
SOLDIER

The Correspondence and Journals of
EDWARD STANLEY ABBOT
1853-1863

Quincy S. Abbot

ABBOT

Published by Quincy S. Abbot
West Hartford, CT

ISBN 978-0-9882109-0-5

Library of Congress Control Number: 2012915627

*To William F. Abbot, my grandfather and
Stanley's little Brother Willie,
whose devotion to family history and
preservation of family documents
both inspired and enabled this book*

CONTENTS

Pictures, Maps, and Drawings

Sources of pictures and drawings:

AA	Abbot Archives
NHS	Norwich Historical Society
WOM	White Oak Museum
YUL	Manuscripts and Archives, Yale University Library
USN	U.S. Naval Historical Center

PREFACE

I write this preface sitting at my grandfather William F. Abbot's 1891 rolltop desk. The top drawer contains a minie ball—a type of rifle bullet—like the one that killed Brother Stanley at Gettysburg in July, 1863. Their older brother, Edwin, picked it up on the battlefield a week after the great battle between North and South. He was there to bring Stanley's body home to Beverly, Massachusetts for burial.

The rolltop desk arrived at our house when I was a boy of eight, along with an early-nineteenth-century Sheraton-style secretary desk stuffed full with family letters, toys, and other heirlooms.[1] Henry Larcom, Stanley's grandfather and a sea captain who lived in Beverly, was the original owner. During my frequent childhood absences from school due to illness—there were no vaccines or antibiotics in the 1930's and 1940's—I liked nothing better than to play with the toys, especially a wooden humming top and Captain Larcom's telescope that had sailed around the world with him. I also enjoyed reading the documents within its drawers—among them, Stanley's journals and correspondence with his mother, Brother Willie, Sister Emmie, and Cousin Emmie.[2]

In 1972, Hurricane Agnes flooded my parents' home in Forty-Fort, Pennsylvania, upended the secretary desk, and stripped it of its veneer. I brought the damaged furniture back to

---

1. The secretary desk and its two matching card tables are now on display at the Beverly Historical Society, Beverly, Massachusetts.
2. Since some of the letter writers spelled the nickname as "Emmy" or used the abbreviated nickname "Em," each such letter reflects the writer's individual preference.

Connecticut for restoration. Once the wood had dried enough to open the drawers, the documents within were spread out across the basement floor to dry. Miraculously, the paper and ink survived, although some of Stanley's letters remain to this day water-stained and mud-coated.

It was only in retirement when I returned to my childhood pursuit of reading the family papers that I rediscovered Stanley, and embarked upon the ten-year-plus process of creating this book. It began as an essay for the family about Stanley's role in the Civil War based on the inherited letters and journals, until I learned that the nearby Yale University Library contained 51.5 linear feet of the "Edwin Hale Abbot Family Papers" in their Manuscripts and Archives center. Thankfully, most of the papers related to Edwin's legal and business activities, and only two feet to personal matters.

The Yale collection enriched my own trove of material, taking it beyond just another war story. It disclosed a mid-nineteenth-century youth's journey to adulthood as Stanley struggled with himself, his siblings, his parents, and the world, on the way to finding his place as a writer and an adult—as well as an officer and a gentleman in the Union Army. Along the way he described his experiences in school, small towns, college, and the Army.

After Stanley's death his commanding officer, who was also a friend of Brother Edwin, described Stanley's character and touched on his habit of letter-writing.

Head Quarters, U.S. Forces
Columbus, Ohio
October 29, 1863

My dear [Edwin] Abbot,
    [Stanley] was a good fellow, and among many temptations, a man of good morals and habits. He neither gambled nor drank, as some of us did. I can probably tell you nothing about him that you do not know except perhaps the depth of his affection for you. He loved you with more than a brother's love. . . .

We used to laugh at him for the long letters he wrote you. I think his account of the battle of Chancellorsville, to which he devoted much time, was the moving cause. His manly (and at the same time boyish in its freshness and honesty) enthusiasm, when he defended his action, is very prominent still in my memory of him. Then we would laugh at his enthusiasm until half angry, half laughing himself, we would tempt him into metaphysics—of which he was very fond.

He had a keen sense of humor too and his cheery laugh (much like his sister, Miss Emmy's) I shall never forget. I never saw him laugh as he did at the story of Dr. Colton, who messed with us, of a California mule who was able to climb hills so steep that they leaned back the other way and this was accounted for by the fact that the mule was so stubborn he would not even obey the laws of gravitation.

Charles Goddard

Stanley left no direct descendants to uncover and tell his story. With the 150th Anniversary of what Stanley considered to be a war to preserve the Union in mind, I compiled this record of his life in the hope that his dream of becoming an acknowledged writer will be realized through these journals and letters. Indeed, he may even have anticipated such posthumous recognition. The second item in Stanley's copybook reads:

I care not whether my work be read now or by posterity. I can afford to wait a century for readers when God himself has waited six thousand years for an observer.

Kepler

The nineteenth-century documents presented many transcription problems. Due to the penurious use of paper, paragraph breaks in the originals are sparse and writing became smaller as the end of the paper approached. The ink and pens of the time made periods and commas indistinguishable from one another. Paragraphs and punctuation are supplied so as to ease the reading experience, but otherwise the quoted material is unaltered. The original of the second journal was not found, but Sister Emily's transcribed excerpts from it were among the family papers and are included here.

Quincy S. Abbot
West Hartford, Connecticut

ACKNOWLEDGEMENTS

I wish to acknowledge the following for their assistance with this book:

> Helen George transcribed the letters and journals by deciphering the handwriting, the archaic words and spellings, and the increasingly minuscule handwriting as the paper started to run out before the thoughts did.

> Nancy Osgood, Norwich Historical Society, provided information about both the town and university at Norwich, Vermont.

> Dennis Champlain, Worthy Image, drew the maps.

> Darren Brown, Beverly Historical Society, provided information about Independence Park.

> Donald Pfanz, Staff Historian, Fredericksburg & Spotsylvania National Military Park, helped me understand the area of Falmouth, Virginia in which Stanley bivouacked during the first six months of 1863.

> E. P. Newton, Curator of the White Oak Civil War Museum in Falmouth, Virginia shed further light on the Falmouth bivouacks.

> Ruth Gonchar Brennan, who has written about her own family, offered valuable suggestions pertaining to the book's structure.

- Charles B. Dew, Ephraim Williams Professor of American History at Williams College, reviewed and verified factual aspects relating to the book's Civil War background.

- Joslyn Pine line edited and copy edited my draft.

- Susan Ahlquist assisted with layout and other preparation of the draft for printing.

- My daughter Susan Pelletier, magazine writer and editor, made this a true family project by reviewing an early draft and engaging in long conversations with me about the book as it progressed.

- George Wingate's incisive observations about the letters enriched the book.

- Cousin Elinor Abbot, a member of the last Abbot generation to be raised at the Abbot Homestead in Wilton, New Hampshire, shared her knowledge of its history and her insights as an anthropologist.

- Distant cousin David Murphy improved immeasurably the photographs of people and Stanley's drawings with his Photoshop expertise, and provided valuable feedback on several drafts of the book.

- Manuscripts and Archives, Yale University Library; Manuscripts and Archives, Andover-Harvard Theological Library, Harvard Divinity School; and Library of Congress allowed access to and reproduction of papers and photographs of family members contained in their files.

- U.S. Naval Historical Center for photo of the *Monitor*.

- My wife, Zelia, listened patiently to my numerous progress reports, in addition to commenting on an early draft.

TIMELINE

OCT. 22, 1841	Stanley born in Boston, Massachusetts
1841–SEPT. 1855	Lived with his parents in Boston while attending Boston Latin School and the private Latin School of E. S. Dixwell, Esq.
SEPT. 1855–1863	Stanley and family lived with Grandfather Henry Larcom in Beverly, Massachusetts
SEPT. 1855–JUNE 1857	Continued at Dixwell's Latin School
AUG. 1857–MID-1859	Stock boy at wholesale druggist, Reed, Cutler & Co., in Boston, Massachusetts
SEPT. 1859–JUNE 1860	Attended Phillips Exeter Academy in Exeter, New Hampshire, to prepare for Harvard[1]
SEPT. 1860–JUNE 1861	Freshman at Harvard in Cambridge, Massachusetts
JULY, 1861–AUG. 1861	Hiked through the White Mountains with his father's friend, John Witt Randall
SEPT. 1861	Began sophomore year at Harvard
SEPT. 1861–NOV. 1861	At home in Beverly when he was threatened with brain fever

---

1. In the nineteenth century, Harvard was sometimes referred to as "University of Cambridge."

Nov. 1861–March 1862	Recuperated at Abbot Homestead in Wilton, New Hampshire
March 1862–June 1862	Attended military classes at Norwich University in Norwich, Vermont
July 1, 1862–Dec. 7, 1862	Training new recruits at Ft. Preble, Portland, Maine
July 1, 1862	Enlisted as a private, 17th U.S. Infantry Regiment at Ft. Preble, Portland, Maine
Oct. 1, 1862	Promoted to Sergeant
Nov. 10, 1862	Commissioned as 2nd Lieutenant, 17th U.S. Infantry Regiment at Ft. Preble, Portland, Maine
Dec. 7, 1862–Dec. 20, 1862	Travelled from Ft. Preble to Falmouth, Virginia, with thirty-eight troops
Dec. 20, 1862	Assigned to Company A, 1st Battalion, 17th U.S. Infantry Regiment, Second Brigade, Second Division, Fifth Corps, Army of the Potomac
Dec. 20, 1862–Jan. 20, 1863	Bivouac at Falmouth, Virginia
Jan. 20, 1863–Jan. 23, 1863	Part of Mud March, a failed attack on Fredericksburg, Virginia
Jan. 23, 1863–April 28, 1863	Bivouac in Falmouth, Virginia
April 27, 1863	Promoted to 1st Lieutenant

APRIL 28, 1863–MAY 7, 1863	Battle of Chancellorsville, Virginia
MAY 7, 1863–JUNE 4, 1863	Bivouac in Falmouth, Virginia
JUNE 4, 1863–JUNE 13, 1863	Part of reserves in Benson's Mills, Virginia, who guarded three fords in the Rappahannock River against a possible attack by Gen. Lee
JUNE 13, 1863–JULY 2, 1863	Marched about 125 miles from Benson's Mills, Virginia, to Gettysburg, Pennsylvania
JULY 2, 1863	Wounded on Houck's Ridge near Little Round Top, Gettysburg, Pennsylvania
JULY 2, 1863	Promoted to Brevet Captain for gallant and meritorious services at Gettysburg
JULY 8, 1863	Died in the Field Hospital at Gettysburg, Pennsylvania; temporary burial in a farmer's field
JULY 23, 1863	Reinterred in Central Cemetery, Beverly, Massachusetts

MILITARY UNITS OF EDWARD STANLEY ABBOT

Unit	Dates	Commanders
Army of the Potomac	July 26, 1861– Nov. 9, 1862	Maj. Gen. George B. McClellan
	Nov. 9, 1862– Jan. 26, 1863	Maj. Gen Ambrose Burnside
	Jan. 26, 1863– June 28, 1863	Maj. Gen. Joseph Hooker
	June 28, 1863–?	Maj. Gen. George G. Meade
Fifth Corps	Nov. 1862– June 28, 1863	Maj. Gen. George G. Meade
	June 28, 1863–?	Maj. Gen. George Sykes
Second Division	1862– June 28, 1863	Maj. Gen. George Sykes
	June 28, 1863–?	Brig. Gen. Romeyn B. Ayres
Second Brigade	Early 1863–?	Col. Sidney Burbank
17th U.S. Regiment	July 1862–?	Lt. Col. J. Durrell Greene
1st Battalion	April 1863–?	Maj. George L. Andrews
Company A	Dec. 1862–?	Capt. Charles Goddard[1]
	July 2, 1863	1st. Lt. David Montgomery
	July 2, 1863	1st Lt. L. Smith

---

1. Capt. Goddard was sick on July 2, 1863 and so he did not participate in the Battle at Gettysburg. Montgomery commanded until wounded, then Smith took over.

Genealogy of Edward Stanley Abbot[1]

1 Samuel Abbot (1786–1839)

1 Abiel Abbot (1765–1859) m. Elizabeth Abbot (1766–1853)

1 Ezra Abbot (1772–1847) m. Rebekah Hale (1781–1860)

   2 Rebecca Abbot (1800–1882) m. Isaac Knight (1797–1850)

      3 Emily Maria Knight (1845–1864)

   2 Joseph Hale Abbot (1802–1873)
m. Fanny Larcom (1807–1883)

      3 Henry Larcom Abbot (1831–1927)
m. Mary Susan Everett (1832–1871)

      3 Edwin Hale Abbot (1834–1927)
m. 1st Martha Carter (1836–1860) and
m. 2nd Martha Trask Steele (1839–1932)

      3 Francis Ellingwood Abbot (1836–1903)
m. Katherine Fearing Loring (1839–1893)

      3 Emily Frances Abbot (1839–1899)
m. Abiel Abbot Vaughan (1839–1907)

      3 **Edward Stanley Abbot (1841–1863)**

      3 William Fitzhale Abbot (1853–1922)
m. Carolyn Ward Sewall (1860–1939)

         4 Theodore Sewall Abbot (1897–1993)
m. Alice Eleanor Howell (1902–1996)

            5 Quincy Sewall Abbot (1932–)
m. Zelia Gillam (1932–)

---

1. This list includes only those family members who play a significant role in the book.

2   Abiel Abbot (1808–1896)

2   Harriet Abbot (1814–1886)
    m. Hermon Abbot (1814–1878)

2   Harris Abbot (1812–1884)
    m. Caroline Ann Butler (1836–1911)

    3   Stanley Harris Abbot (1863–1935)

    3   Charles Greeley Abbot (1872–1973)

2   Nelson Abbot (1816–1891)
    m. Hannah Holt Pevey (1821–1891)

2   John Hale Abbot (1825–1905)

Key:

1 = grandparent's generation

2 = parent's generation (Stanley's uncles and aunts)

3 = Stanley's generation (Stanley's siblings and first cousins)

4 = Stanley's next generation (nephew)

5 = Stanley's second next generation (grandnephew)

CHAPTER 1

A YOUTH'S DILEMMA

Nothing is here for tears, nothing to wail
Or knock the breast; no weakness; no contempt,
Dispraise, or blame; nothing but well and fair,
And what may quiet us in a death so noble.
—JOHN MILTON, *Samson Agonistes*

Fourscore and seven years after the death of his great grand-uncle Nathan Hale, Edward Stanley Abbot (Stanley) died in the midst of his efforts to preserve the union that Nathan Hale had died to create.[1] Stanley and his family were well aware of their patriotic heritage. Indeed, Father Joseph Hale Abbot (Hale) in 1833 transmitted to writer Jared Sparks "a few particulars communicated to me by the late General Hull of Newton in the year 1823 not contained in the account of Capt. Nathan Hale written by him & inserted in Miss Hannah Adams's *Hist. of New England*."[2]

In spite of this heritage, his parents opposed Stanley joining the Army. He felt free to discuss the situation only with his two-year-older Sister Emily in a letter written eight months after the attack on Ft. Sumter started the Civil War.

---

1. Stanley's great grandfather, Joseph Hale, was a brother of Nathan Hale. Joseph Hale's daughter, Rebekah Hale, married Stanley's grandfather, Ezra Abbot.
2. Hannah Adams, *A Summary History of New England* (Dedham: Self-published, 1799). A draft of this letter is in the Abbot Archives.

1

Wilton [New Hampshire]
December 15, 1861

Dear [Sister] Em,

Secretiveness is the rule of our family. I wish to prove that rule by making an exception to it. . . . They don't trust me much at home. . . . They think I want to be a 'gay soldier boy.' It is really hard and bitter to know that Mother thinks I am so boyish. Henry, of course, doesn't know much of me and Edwin is a creedist and thinks they are going wrong whose faces are not turned to the New Church. . . ."

I, in my heart, believe that the cause for which this war is undertaken is a just and politic one, that it needs a million hands to carry it on, and that every man that is free from the burden of supporting others ought to give up his time, the furtherance of his own plans, and, if need be, his life to help in assuring the ultimate triumph of this cause.

The question we have to decide is simply this: shall America in the coming centuries, when her children are numbered by hundreds of millions, be desolated by long and bloody wars such as have been the agony and have assured the slavery of Europe since her history began? I for one say "No." It can be avoided by maintaining one great empire through the length and breadth of the continent. To maintain this empire is worth their every sacrifice it is within the power of the people to make. No price that can be paid is too high, and now the question comes up, can we maintain the cause for which we are fighting? Have we the physical power to do that? I own I am in painful doubt.

I fear the chances are against us. At any rate, if we do succeed, it will be after a struggle more bitter and desperate than any recorded in history. It will be by the exercise of every power we are master of. Every man that can strike a blow will be bitterly missed if he dare not come forward in his country's time of agony—I cannot be such a man, Em. I think it is a glorious thing when one has a chance to be a hero.

I used to read, when I was a little boy, of brave and noble men and wish that I might be a brave and noble man myself. . . . The possibility of becoming such is offered once to each and all. Woe to him that dare not grasp at the prize when it is within his reach.[3]

⎯⎯⎯⎯⎯

Stanley left school at the age of fifteen to work for a wholesale druggist in Boston. It was a menial, physically demanding job, packing and delivering boxes of Cutler's Vegetable Pulmonary Balsam and other products. After a year and a half, he quit. While there was talk in the air about slavery and states rights, war was not yet accepted as inevitable when this seventeen-year-old sat on a beach in the summer of 1859 developing a dream for his future. Stanley reflected on that particular time four years later, following a boring three-month bivouac in Virginia:

> Camp Sykes Division
> March 28, 1863
>
> Dear [Sister] Emmie,
>   Have you curiosity to know the future I had chalked out for myself? It was this, very humble, with the clink of no money in it. One day before I went to Exeter[4] to prepare for college I went down to the seashore to an old revolutionary redoubt from whence in times gone by 3 guns had frowned upon the pretty bay at the head of which nestled the sleepy town of Beverly [Massachusetts.]
>   I curled myself up under the grassy rampart and looked out on the water on which the dazzling sunlight lay, fashioning in my mind the life I would live. I would go to college and learn how to think and write. I would get some teacher's place in a country academy and make the distasteful drudgery of 6 hours earn the bread for 24 and, bye and bye, when I was thirty years old and more,

---

3. The complete text of the letter to Emmie from Stanley dated December 15, 1861 is on page 97.
4. Stanley entered Phillips Exeter Academy in the fall of 1859 to prepare himself for Harvard.

I would begin in leisure moments to write things that
somehow I felt would be in my heart to say.[5]

Stanley, like most teenagers, struggled to grow up, but his
struggles were against Brother Edwin rather than his father,
who had a relatively small role in his life. However, Stanley
was unusually cognizant of the internal dimensions of his
struggle. He wrote his brother Edwin on October 30, 1860:

> I took refuge in silence. I wish you clearly to
> understand that the struggle for freedom was not with
> you. It was with myself and when I pained you, as I often
> did by showing what you thought a dogged disposition to
> reject your advice on all matters, I in reality was so utterly
> miserable in resisting you that, when I spoke to you most
> sharply and cruelly, I longed most to throw my arms round
> your neck and cry for your forgiveness.

Stanley's journals and correspondence demonstrate through
his own words and those of his correspondents, the geographi-
cal journey and emotional growth he experienced as he struggled with himself, his family and the world, to become an adult,
a soldier, and, ultimately, a brave and noble man who sacri-
ficed his life for his country.

---

5. See letter to Cousin Mattie from Stanley dated March 28, 1863 on
   page 189.

—∞∞—

CHAPTER 2

FAMILY AND PLACES IN STANLEY'S LIFE

We owe it to our ancestors to preserve entire those rights, which
they have delivered to our care: we owe it to our posterity, not
to suffer their dearest inheritance to be destroyed.

—JUNIUS, *Letters*

Family

Stanley was a New Englander to the core, blending his father's
heritage of inland farming with the legacy of his mother's
coastal upbringing. Most of his ancestors arrived in New England during the Great Migration from England before 1642.
Stanley was the fifth of six children surviving birth. He had
three older brothers (Henry, Edwin, and Francis), a younger
brother (William), and an older sister (Emily).

While his mother was an only child, his father was the
third of thirteen children. Since the firstborn was a daughter,
and the second was a son who died unnamed during child-
birth, his father grew up as the oldest son. Stanley knew
well the uncles, aunts and cousins on his father's side from
visits to the Abbot Homestead on Abbot Hill in Wilton, New
Hampshire.

Father Joseph Hale Abbot (Hale) was descended from
a New England farming family with a scientific bent. After
residing for over a century in Andover, Massachusetts, his for-
bears moved to Wilton in the 1760's. In true Yankee fashion,

JOSEPH HALE ABBOT
1802–1873

Grandfather Ezra Abbot, together with his Brother Samuel, developed the first mill to turn potatoes into starch, a higher value product that was easier to transport to the city markets.[1] This was the Yankee equivalent of turning corn into liquor for easy transport to markets from the mountains of Appalachia.

Hale was a teacher with broad interests. He taught Latin and modern languages at Bowdoin College in Brunswick, Maine, following his graduation there. He taught mathematics and natural philosophy at Phillips Exeter Academy, lectured to the general public at the Boston Athenæum in experimental chemistry and natural sciences, served as secretary of the American Academy of Arts and Sciences, founded a girls' school in Boston, and was the first principal of the high school in Beverly, Massachusetts.[2] However, Hale related poorly to his own teenage son, Stanley, and opposed his joining the Army.

Mother Fanny Ellingwood Larcom was descended from a New England seafaring family.[3] She grew up in Beverly, Massachusetts, on Cape Ann, north of Boston. Her father and many Larcom ancestors were merchants or seamen or both. Fanny was an educated woman having attended both formal and informal schools as a youth, and she continued to be an avid reader as an adult. In later years, she published stories, primarily about her family and her surroundings, including one in the *Atlantic Monthly* entitled "My Father's Shipwreck."[4] Fanny's half-second cousin, Lucy Larcom, also

---

1. J. Almus Russell, "Found: Site of the First Starch Mill," *Yankee*, October, 1969, 34–43.
2. Maj. Lemuel Abijah Abbott, *Descendants of George Abbott of Rowley, Massachusetts* (Boston: Self-published, 1906), 687–688.
3. Fanny is occasionally addressed by Hale in letters not in this book as "Frances." This may account for Daughter Emily "Frances" Abbot and Son "Francis" Ellingwood Abbot. However, the name "Fanny" is documented as the name of Grandmother Fanny Ellingwood and Granddaughter Fanny Larcom Abbot.
4. Fanny Larcom Abbot, "My Father's Shipwreck," *Atlantic Monthly*, August, 1871, 144–160.

FANNY LARCOM ABBOT
1807–1883

from Beverly, was a well-known writer of books and poetry about New England.

Brother Henry Larcom Abbot (Henry), ten years older than Stanley, was married with a child when the War began. An 1854 West Point graduate, Henry had already distinguished himself by working on the Pacific Railroad Survey in California and Oregon, and on a survey of the Mississippi River's water flow from the Ohio River to the Gulf of Mexico. Henry had not lived near his parental home since before Stanley was born. As a result, he did not know his little brother well. Nonetheless, he helped support Stanley financially in preparatory school and college, and recommended to his officer colleagues—who were also his friends—that Stanley be appointed a lieutenant in the Regular Army.

Brother Edwin Hale Abbot (Ed or Eddie), seven years older than Stanley, graduated from Harvard in 1855. He became a tutor in classical languages at Harvard from 1857 to 1862, while studying for his law degree, and later entered into private practice in Boston. Edwin was like a father to his younger brother, guiding his decisions and assisting in the finances for Stanley's education—as well as being the object of his teenage rebellion. Their correspondence and relationship form a substantial part of Stanley's story.

Brother Francis Ellingwood Abbot (Frank), five years older than Stanley, graduated from Harvard in 1859—the same year he married—and immediately enrolled in Harvard Divinity School. Shortly thereafter he transferred to Meadville Theological School in Pennsylvania. Frank, while at home and later at Harvard, was a close confidant of Stanley, but the contact was limited after Frank moved to Meadville. It is clear that a close relationship endured despite their contact being limited to letters, with Frank offering young Stanley brotherly advice.

Sister Emily Frances Abbot (Em or Emmie), two years older than Stanley, was educated at Hale's school for girls. She lived at home when the War Between the States began, but frequently her letters described activities while visiting friends,

Brother Frank, or other relatives. Since she was the closest to his age, Stanley knew Emmie the best of his siblings. Consequently, he felt free to share his thoughts and feelings with her. She preserved these letters from Stanley and passed them along to Brother Willie on her death.

Edward Stanley Abbot (Stanley) was born on October 22, 1841, the fifth of six children surviving birth. His older brother Edwin had preempted the nickname "Eddie," so Stanley was known by his middle name. His letters and journals contain many reflections about nature and the world around him, and he aspired to be a writer when he grew up. From the age of fifteen onward, he engaged in regular correspondence with siblings and cousins, and maintained a personal journal from time to time.

Brother William Fitzhale Abbot (Willie), twelve years younger than Stanley, was an eight-year-old when the War began. Willie revered and respected his older brother, who demonstrated a love for the younger brother by spending time with him while at home playing soldiers and other games, and later writing to Willie about a soldier's life and instructing him on military exercises that Willie could engage in with his toy soldiers.

First cousin Emily Maria Knight (Emmie) was a daughter of Rebecca Abbot Knight, a sister of Stanley's father. Emmie was three years younger than Stanley. After her father died in 1850, Emmie and her mother returned to the Abbot Homestead in Wilton, New Hampshire to live there with Emmie's grandmother and Uncle Harris.[5] Stanley played with Emmie during his boyhood visits to the Abbot Homestead. Following Emily's death in 1864, Stanley's letters to her while he was attending Dixwell's Latin School and when he worked for Reed, Cutler & Co. in Boston were returned to his mother and form a major portion of Chapter 3.

---

5. Wilton's census data from 1850 and 1860 suggests that Emily and her mother had moved elsewhere by the time of Stanley's extended visit there in 1861–1862.

Third cousin Martha Trask Steele (Mattie) was two years older than Stanley and lived in Portland, Maine.[6] Stanley's infatuation with Mattie, which started at the age of eight, was revived while he was stationed at Ft. Preble in Portland Harbor where he enlisted in the Army. They corresponded frequently after Stanley transferred to Virginia. Stanley's letters to her were found with Brother Edwin's papers.

A Military Tradition

Service in the militia was native to Colonial New England life, whether it transpired on land in the Indian wars on Stanley's paternal side or at sea against the pirates on his mother's side. The custom continued with his family's involvement in the Revolutionary War.

Great grandfather Lieutenant Joseph Hale responded to the call for help on April 19, 1775. He participated in the siege of Boston which followed the battles of Lexington and Concord, and later served in Captain Knowlton's Company, Putnam's Regiment. According to the family lore, he contracted consumption[7] following his imprisonment on one of the infamous Jersey prison ships, and it caused his death a few years later.[8] Great grandfather Captain Abiel Abbot fought in the Revolutionary War at the Battle of White Plains.[9]

Great grandfather Henry Larcom, Sr. was a Second Lieutenant, second in command of the schooner *Scorpion*, a privateer during the Revolutionary War. In 1780, he died of "ship fever"—probably typhus—shortly after returning home from

---

6. They had common second great grandparents, John Abbot and Phoebe Fiske of Andover, Massachusetts.
7. Consumption is today known as pulmonary tuberculosis. http://en.wikipedia.org/wiki/Tuberculosis. Last updated June 9, 2012.
8. George Dudley Seymour, *Captain Nathan Hale, Major John Palsgrave Wyllys: A Digressive History* (New Haven: Self-published), 18.
9. Abbott, *Descendants of George Abbott*, 270.

captivity on "the Old Jersey Prison ship near New York City."[10] Grandfather Henry Larcom, Jr. had a ship seized by Napoleon's navy in 1810, and the ship bringing him home was wrecked in a storm: "In this small and shattered boat three of us had lived twenty-three days, since leaving the wreck and on the 21st of July we arrived safely at G[loucester], and in a short time reached our respective families, to the mutual joy of ourselves and our friends."[11] A rope measuring his waist at the time of rescue, now residing with the Henry L. Abbot Papers at the Library of Congress, measures only twenty-one inches.

Finally, there is Stanley's great granduncle Nathan Hale, who is often quoted as saying in reference to his fate in the Revolutionary War, "I only regret that I have but one life to lose for my country." The quote is believed to have derived from the play *Cato* (1712) by British dramatist Joseph Addison. With its strong political overtones that had much in common with the themes of the American Revolution, it became especially popular with the Founding Fathers, making it likely to be a play with which Nathan was familiar.[12] The language in the play that closely corresponds to the quote is found in Act Four, Scene II: "What pity is it, that we can die but once, to serve our country!"[13] Nathan Hale's actual statement is now thought to be: "I am so satisfied with the cause in which I have engaged, that my only regret is, that I have not more lives than one to offer in its service."[14]

Stanley's feelings about the Civil War were that "Every man that is free from the burden of others ought to give up his

---

10. William F. Abbot, "Genealogy of the Larcom Family," in *The Essex Institute Historical Collections,* vol. 58, nos. 1 and 2 (1922), 142.

11. Abbot, "My Father's Shipwreck," 150.

12. http://en.wikipedia.org/wiki/Cato_a_tragedy. Last updated June 2, 2012.

13. Project Gutenberg eBook of *Cato,* 2010.

14. Frank Moore, *Diary of the American Revolution: From Newspapers to Original Documents,* vol. II (New York: Charles Scribner, 1860), 429.

time, the furtherance of his own plans, and, if need be, his life to help in assuring the ultimate triumph of this cause."[15] Each made the ultimate sacrifice to achieve the same goal—the creation and preservation of an independent and united nation. Stanley had his own unique perspective, but it expressed essentially the same love and pride of country as great granduncle Nathan's.

Places in Stanley's Life

Boston, Massachusetts. Stanley was born, lived, and attended school until his mid-teens in Boston, "which I always have regarded and always shall regard as my real home."[16]

Beverly, Massachusetts. Stanley's maternal grandparents, Henry and Fanny Larcom, lived in Beverly about seventeen miles from Boston. As a child, Stanley visited them frequently. When he was fourteen, the family moved to Beverly to live with Grandfather Larcom who was then a widower. But Stanley could not be happy there. A letter from Edwin to Stanley on September 29, 1862 notes that, "Even Mother says it will not do for you to come to Beverly any more to stay at present, both because father finds money so hard to get that he cannot afford it and because you are not careful enough to treat him with due respect and to control yourself in his company."

Wilton, New Hampshire. Stanley's paternal grandparents, Ezra and Rebekah Hale Abbot, and other relatives lived at and farmed the Abbot Homestead on Abbot Hill in Wilton, a small town in southern New Hampshire. "How strange it seems to come to Wilton, and seemingly take up the life and thoughts of

---

15. See letter to Sister Emily from Stanley dated December 15, 1861 on page 97.
16. See letter to Mother from Stanley dated September 29, 1860 on page 55.

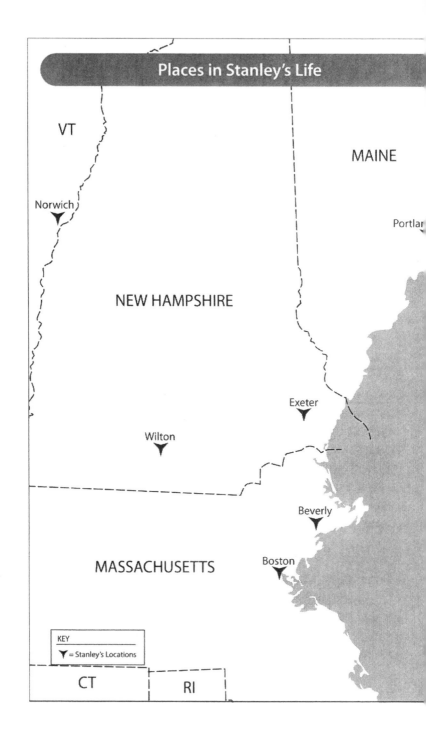

Places in Stanley's Life

VT

MAINE

Norwich

Portlar

NEW HAMPSHIRE

Exeter

Wilton

Beverly

Boston

MASSACHUSETTS

KEY

▼ = Stanley's Locations

CT

RI

years gone by!"[17] mused Stanley in his journal when he sought
refuge there from illness at the beginning of his sophomore
year in college. On today's highways, the drive from Boston or
Beverly to Wilton is only one and a half hours. In the middle
of the nineteenth century, the trip was much longer. Stanley's
uncle Harris describes a trip from Boston back to Wilton in a
letter to Stanley's parents.

> Wilton, New Hampshire
> July 16, 1847
>
> Dear Brother and Sister,
>   I arrived in season for the [railroad] cars, procured
> a ticket for Lowell [Massachusetts], and reached there
> between 3 and 4 o'clock, spent the time until 5 o'clock in
> doing business and making calls upon friends. I rode in the
> cars to Nashua [New Hampshire] and thence in the stage
> by way of Amherst to Milford arriving there about ½ past
> 9 P.M. I intended to walk home from Milford." [The walking
> distance is about 11 miles.]
>
> Yours affectionately,
> Harris

Exeter, New Hampshire. Stanley attended Phillips Exeter
Academy for one year to prepare for Harvard: "[The town of]
Exeter is such a dull old hole that a week here is equal to a
year anywhere else."[18] However, he could find pleasure there
in unexpected ways, as he did while on a visit to an old friend
of his mother: "I went and much to my astonishment I enjoyed
myself."[19] Visits home were easy since Exeter was only a short
forty-mile train trip from Beverly.

Norwich, Vermont. Stanley attended Norwich University for
military training. He described Norwich to his mother in a

---

17. See Stanley's journal, November 23, 1861 in on page 93.
18. See letter to Mother from Stanley dated March 4, 1860 on page 45.
19. See letter to Edwin from Stanley dated October 25, 1859 on page 42.

letter written April 15, 1862: *"Tout arrive en France,* they say. Surely then, Norwich is the antipodes of France for nothing happens here." Even so, he "made the acquaintance of a jolly old farmer by the name of Hazen, who is really quite a character."[20] Norwich was on the Connecticut River, a good distance from Wilton.

---

20. See letter to Edwin from Stanley dated April 26, 1862 on page 132.

CHAPTER 3

THE SCHOOLBOY AND THE GREENHORN
OCTOBER, 1853–APRIL, 1859

Being moody, defiant, impulsive, confused, depressed, anxious, and overwhelmed are all part of being a young person. Trying to discover "Who am I?" is also normal.
—*HopeWorks* newsletter, SPRING 2010

Stanley's family settled in Boston in September, 1833, where Father Joseph Hale Abbot became well regarded for his school for girls and for his scientific lectures at the Boston Athenæum. His sons, including Stanley, received a first rate education at Boston Latin School and Dixwell's Latin School. Then, in 1855, "owing to a severe attack of sciatica," Hale gave up his school and the family moved to Beverly to live with Grandfather Henry Larcom, while Stanley commuted by train to continue at Mr. Dixwell's school in Boston.[1]

In the autumn of 1856, Father Hale returned alone "to Boston . . . where he received some private pupils and pursued his favorite studies in Natural Science" while the family remained in Beverly with Grandfather Larcom.[2] Hale continued in Boston until 1861, reopening his school for a year

---

1. William F. Abbot, *Joseph Hale Abbot: A Memorial Tribute by His Youngest Son* (Boston: Self-published, 1890), 173.
2. Ibid.

HENRY LARCOM HOUSE
BEVERLY, MASSACHUSETTS

and working on definitions of scientific terms for *Worcester's Dictionary*.[3] During this time he was distant both physically and emotionally from the rest of the family. Meanwhile, Henry and Edwin were responsible for the financial support of Fanny and the younger children (Stanley, Emmie and Willie) in Beverly. Together, the family dislocations and his separation from his father had profound effects on Stanley during his critical teenage years. Thus, Stanley's childhood ended, and the written record began in Boston as Edwin mused about his brother, who was nearly twelve years old by this time. It foreshadowed an ongoing concern for his younger sibling that persisted throughout Stanley's short life.

---

3. "Joseph Emerson Worcester was an American lexicographer who was the chief competitor to Noah Webster of *Webster's Dictionary* in the mid-nineteenth-century. Their rivalry became known as the 'dictionary wars.'" http://en.wikipedia.org/wiki/Joseph Emerson Worcester. Last updated May 27, 2012. Hale produced definitions of scientific terms for the 1860 edition of *Worcester's Dictionary*.

EDWIN'S JOURNAL

October 9, 1853. Stanley troubles me. He is growing up to be a self-willed child. He would not go to church this morning in spite of all I could do to induce him. He is getting lax too on the subject of truth. I do not mean that he would tell a deliberate lie, but that he quibbles . . . and exaggerates in such a way that it will lead him to absolute falsehood, if he is not careful.

After Stanley moved to Beverly, he commuted by train to Dixwell's Latin School in Boston and later to work at a wholesale druggist in Boston. During those years he wrote extensively to his cousin Emily Knight who was three years younger and his playmate from the time he vacationed at the Abbot Homestead in Wilton, New Hampshire.

Beverly
October 23, 1856

Dear [Cousin] Emmie,

Yesterday was my birthday (Mind you not the day I was born but the day I was fifteen years old.) I am sitting tonight in the North Room at Beverly with nothing in particular to do having got my lesson in the afternoon, and I thought I would fulfill the promise that I made to you. Almost every evening my eyes ache so much that I cannot read or write, and I do not get down to Beverly till about half past two in the afternoon so that I do not have much time to write any letters as I have to learn my lessons in the afternoon.

I hope that you will excuse the blots, the writing, and the thoughts embodied therein, as my paper is bad, my pen is worse, and my patience grows less as my letter draws nearer to its close.

Your affectionate cousin,
Stanley

EMILY MARIA KNIGHT
1845–1864

Beverly
February 22, 1857

Dear [Cousin] Emmie,

The boys at school were very much afraid that Mr. Dixwell would not be patriotic enough to give [a holiday on] Washington's Birthday but much to our relief he [con]cluded to let us have the day so that at present, Sunday afternoon, I have the pleasant prospect of a holyday on Monday before me. You asked me in your last letter to send you some more conundrums. I heard the most ridiculous one imaginable the other day, which is almost too silly to send. "Why was Noah the worst rat catcher in the world"? Because it was forty days and forty nights before he lighted on Ararat (ere a rat). . . .

Mr. Dixwell is going to give a party to the school boys on Monday evening but I do not think I shall go as he lives at Cambridge and it would be inconvenient to get into Boston late in the evening. I should like to go very much but on the whole it would seem like putting one's head into the lion's mouth to go to a party given by one's schoolmaster.

Love to all,
Stanley

Brother Frank lived for a time in Concord, boarding with Henry David Thoreau's mother and substituting as a teacher for Franklin Sanborn at the private school there while Sanborn was off assisting John Brown, the militant abolitionist. Sanborn was a social scientist and a memorialist for the American Transcendentalist movement.[4] He was also a member of the "Committee of Six" that funded John Brown.[5] Frank freely gave advice to his younger brother, as well as shared tales about life with the Thoreaus.

---

4. http://www.concordlibrary.org/scollect/fin_aids/F_B_Sanborn.htm. Last updated September 3, 2011.
5. http://en.wikipedia.org/wiki/Franklin_Sanborn. Last updated February 8, 2011.

Concord
February 25, 1857

Dear Stanley,

I am getting tired of boarding at the house of the metaphysical Thoreaus. . . . For supper they invariably have seed-cakes whose only objection is that they are confoundedly aged; in fact, most superlatively seedy.[6]

Affectionately, your brother,
F. E. Abbot

———

Cambridge
March 27, 1857

Dear Stanley,

I do not like to have you complain of not being able to find a "true friend." Everyone capable of true friendship will sooner or later meet a "true friend," yes, more than one. But if you will believe me, you can never find so true ones elsewhere, as in your own home. You had better make your own sister a friend, for you will never have any other half so true and devoted as she. The older you grow, the more you will prize her love, if you learn to prize that which is most valuable on earth, affection. Of course, you know that a mother is the best friend a man can ever have. If you cannot find friends at home, depend upon it, you will look in vain for them in the world after you leave home. But I am not going to sermonize. Do not laugh at what I have already said.

Yours affectionately,
Frank E. Abbot

———

6. A seed cake is a traditional British concoction. The seed cake may be very rich and may contain raisins and currants as well as caraway seeds.

Cambridge
May 16, 1857

Dear Stanley,

You know Katie is coming to B[oston] at recess, and I wish very much that you would try and be pleasant all the time to everybody, so that she may have a pleasant time.[7] You must make her another sister. You are growing up to be a "big boy" now, and we ought to lay aside all "little boyish" difficulties and jealousies now. Let us never more have any at all. We used to "pick" on each other once, you know, but I hope that we shall no longer indulge in that amiable amusement. Before long I suppose you will be a head taller than I am, and it would not look well for us then to "tear each other's eyes out," eh? I believe all children quarrel, but I hate to see childish quarrels last beyond childhood. But there goes recitation bell. Goodbye.

Frank

One consequence of the financial pressures on the family was that Stanley dropped out of school in 1857 and commenced work at a wholesale druggist, Reed, Cutler & Co., located at 33 and 34 India Street, Boston. The Massachusetts *Sun* on April 2, 1857 carried an advertisement for Cutler's Vegetable Pulmonary Balsam which stated that it is "one of the best remedies for Coughs, Colds, and all Pulmonary complaints, ever offered to the public." Stanley probably packaged and delivered to the post office many boxes of the balsam. That he was discontented with the position, however, is obvious from his letters.

Boston
August 21, 1857

Dear [Sister] Emmie,

The eventful Monday morning came at last, on which I was to make my first appearance in "the store." Nothing remarkable happened until I got to Boston. It seemed so

---

7. Katharine Loring (Katie) and Frank were engaged to be married. Frank was an undergraduate at Harvard at the time.

funny to go a way that did not lead to school! I almost instinctively turned up Sudbury St. Without going into particulars, I managed at length to get to the store. I stopped for a moment on the threshold and then walked with quaking steps across the store into the Counting Room. There I found Mr. George Cutler, one of the partners. He asked pleasantly enough if I was ready to go to work, and then conducted me up a pair of narrow stairs into the room above.

There I saw quite a number of men and boys at work. Mr. Cutler told one of the latter to show me where to put my clothes. So off we trotted as fast as our legs would carry us. Presently after going up several pairs of stairs we reached a place where there were lots of boxes all stuck up on end when we arrived. There my companion acquainted me with the fact that there was no box for me but "that, as a special favour, you may put your clothes in my box for today, that is if they are clean," said he.

And then without giving me time to answer, he asked me if I was a "greenhorn." I told him that I thought "I had better go right downstairs for I was afraid my ears would take to growing if I staid there much longer." He stared at first and then laughed and said he did not mean to call me any names but that was what they called unhappy individuals who had never been in any store, which somewhat soothed me for I had begun to grow excited.

When I had put on my clothes I went downstairs. A man down there set me to putting up bundles which occupied me the whole forenoon. At about two I went and got my dinner and did up bundles again in the afternoon just as I did in the morning. When night came I went home tired. Oh! How tired! For the first few days my feet were very sore but they are well now.

Your affectionate brother,
Stanley

Wilton
August 22, 1857

Dear Stanley,

I was delighted to hear Emily read your letter last evening. It was a treat to me to leave home at this time on account of your and Edwin's plans. I have enjoyed myself very well since I left home, because it has been pleasant to see old friends and old haunts, which are associated with some of my happiest days. . . .

I was glad to learn the history of that "first day at the store" and I augur good from it. How precious our evenings will be this winter if we are permitted to pass them together. . . .

Emily Knight has grown very tall, and appears in good health. She has to help her mother almost all the time and would be glad, as you would I think, to have a good play week.

Love to all
from yr. aff. Mother

———

Beverly
August 26, 1857

Dear Mother,

I don't know as there is anything new that I can tell you about the store for all I have had to do as yet is packing up bundles, weighing out drugs and last, but by no manner of means least, running of errands. In this way I spend my days, and my evenings when I am not too, too tired . . . either in reading or in writing letters. Today I have been at work in the store say perhaps twenty minutes and all the rest of the time has been occupied in going on errands! But this is an exception not a rule.

Your affectionate son,
Stanley

A letter to Cousin Emmie on October 10, 1857 starts with a cartoon before the salutation.

No. 33 & 34 India Street, Boston

LEFT: ESA goes in search of some chlorate of lime. MIDDLE: ESA finds the object of his search and it being almost empty determines to tip it up on its side. RIGHT: ESA succeeds in tipping the chlorate of lime and himself too.

> The above [cartoon] is in answer to a question of yours "whether I like my business as well as at first."
>
> Your affectionate cousin,
> Stanley

A letter to Sister Emmie is dated the same day.

> Beverly
> October 10, 1857

Dear [Sister] Emmie,

Tell Uncle Abiel that he went away from Beverly the first day I was sick and called at the store on the last day of my confinement for I went to Boston on the next Monday. I have had the dysentery, not very severely but enough so to confine me to my bed two weeks and to the house four. I have got over that business pretty well and I have a bad cold which troubles not a little.

The hard times don't affect the people in the country, I suppose, so much as they do those in the cities. The state of the money market is the absorbing object of interest in Boston now. New failures are announced every day and some of the largest firms in the city have broken down business. Men say they have never seen anything like it, not even in '37. But little business is done at the store this autumn though the fall is usually the busiest time of the whole year.

Your affectionate brother,
Stanley

Stanley's daily routine is depicted in "Scenes in the Life of Stanley A." They are undated and are addressed on the backside, "For Miss Emily M. Knight."

Scenes in the Life of Stanley A.

LEFT: In bed. RIGHT: Eating breakfast in a hurry.

LEFT: Running for the cars. RIGHT: Going to Boston in the cars.

LEFT: Arrives at "the store." "Cold weather." RIGHT: Effects a change in his apparel.

All hands warm up before going to work. Tremendous cold!!

The footsteps of Mr. Cutler are heard ascending the stairs. The effect is enlivening in the extreme.

By the fall of 1857, it was clear that Hale's return to work in Boston did not provide enough funds to support the family, even with the help from Stanley's job. The older brothers, Henry (H. L.) and Edwin (E. H.), undertook to provide for the mother and children as set forth in a formal legal agreement between the older brothers and their father. Under a separate agreement, Henry and Edwin agreed to loan money to Hale for his support. Note that, in spite of scarce funds, a servant is considered a necessary part of current expenses for the family.

Boston
October 28, 1857

It is agreed between J. H. Abbot, and E. H. and H. L. Abbot that the current expenses of the following members of the family, to wit Mother, Emily, Stanley, Willie, and the servant shall be met by H. L. and E. H. Abbot so long as this contract shall remain in force.

A few months later, Stanley reported to Cousin Emmie on his life away from the store.

Beverly
January 24, 1858

Dear [Cousin] Emmie,

How did I spend the Christmas Holidays?—In the first place I only had Christmas day and that I spent lying on the parlor sofa reading novels. Very different, I imagine, from the way in which you passed your two or three week vacation. Slack-a-daisy! I shall have to say goodbye to almost all vacations now I suppose. "Do I read much"— that depends on what you call reading much. I read on an average one book a week, sometimes more and sometimes, though rarely, less. About that book "Hot Corn"[8]—I have never read it but I know enough of its general character to advise you not to read it. It is a bad book, or at least has

8. Solon Robinson and N. Orr, illus. *Hot Corn: Life Scenes in New York Illustrated, including, the Story of Little Katy, Madalina, the Rag-Picker's Daughter, Wild Maggie, etc.* (New York: De Witt and Davenport, 1854).

the reputation of being so, and it is very certain that no book gets such a name as that has without in a greater or less degree deserving it.

> Give love to all from your
> affectionate coz,
> Edwardus Stanlius Archimandus

A month later Stanley started a letter to Cousin Emmie with more sketches about his life above the salutation.

More Scenes in the Life of Stanley A.

ESA walks down Long Wharf on a windy and rainy day.

One of the "boys" catches hold of ESA as he is starting down "for fun."

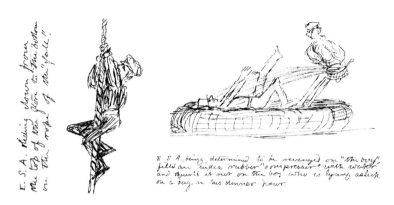

E. S. A. sliding down from the top of the store to the bottom on the rope of the "fall."

E. S. A. being determined to be revenged on "the boy" fills an India rubber "compressor" with water and squirts it out on the boy who is lying asleep on a bag in his dinner hour.

LEFT: ESA sliding down from the top of the store to the bottom on the rope of the "fall." RIGHT: ESA determined to be revenged on "the boy" fills an India rubber "compressor" with water and squirts it out on the boy who is lying asleep on his dinner hour.

> Beverly
> February 28, 1858

Dear [Cousin] Emmie,

Mother and [Sister] Emily went to Boston about the middle of the week and stayed a day or two. I believe Emmie had to go to the dentist's. What a pleasant time she must have had! I believe that if there is one class of men, who, more than any other deserve the extraction and hatred of the rest of mankind, it is that of dentists! Only think of having a great pair of iron nippers thrust into one's mouth, of being tugged and pulled about as if a small steam engine were attached to one's teeth and finally of having a bloody fang thrust almost into one's eyes, a smile of diabolical exultation appearing at the same time on the countenance of the tormentor, as if he were bent on "adding insult to injury." All this is unpleasant but it is nothing to the horror one feels when this fiend in human shape, this dentist, names a day some three months distant when you must return to "his office" and have the pullings, torturings and insults all over again!

> Yours truly,
> Stanley

Stanley's first expression of political thought surfaced in mid-1858 while he was still working at the store.

> Beverly
> June 13, 1858
>
> Dear [Cousin] Emmie,
>
> I have your letter open before me and I see a little interrogation mark at the end of a line, placed there to ascertain if I am much interested in politics. After asking this question you go on to state your very moderate wishes "for your country." "All I care about it is to have peace and no slavery. I don't care who is President if he only does right."
>
> The only difficulty is that everyone does not do right, that there is a civil war in Kansas and Utah, that Slavery is much more likely to be established on Abbot Hill [Wilton, New Hampshire] than to be abolished in So. Carolina, and that it is an even chance, to make the best of it, whether Old Buck does right or wrong.[9] When your wishes come to pass please write me a letter and date it "Wilton Elysium. 180,000,000,000 *ad infinitum.*"
>
> Your affectionate cousin,
> Stanley

—⁂—

> Beverly
> October 17, 1858
>
> Dear [Sister] Emmie,
>
> There is no news to tell you. There never is any. It seems to me, everything goes on in the regular way. The comet grew big and then grew small, likewise the moon. I go into Boston in the morning and come out at night, get up in the morning and go to bed at night, "sing song, ding dong and so the world wags round."
>
> Your affectionate brother,
> Stanley

---

9. "Old Buck" is a reference to President James Buchanan, who held office from 1857–1861.

After working eighteen months at Cutler's, Stanley tired of the job and vigorously sought another position. A first thought was to go to sea but Edwin insisted he consider other options.

Beverly
February 14, 1859

Dear Edwin,

I have thought over what you said to me the other evening and I see no practicable plan that I think I should like better. It is much more promising than the sea project which seems the only alternative, so the sooner we set about carrying it into effect the better. I wish, when you write, you would ask Uncle John how much knowledge of bookkeeping etc. will be required.[10] I suppose I shall have to study that before I start, shall I not?

Your affectionate brother,
Stanley

———

Beverly
February 17, 1859

Dear Edwin,

You say it would be madness to give up a certain occupation for a doubtful chance of one. By this you imply that on the failure of my Western project, I should make up my mind to stay at the store. This, for reasons I have given you, I shall never consent to do, but shall adopt the only alternative, that of going to sea. . . . If he says there is no opening for me there, I shall hunt up a vessel as soon as possible and begin to support myself. If, on the contrary, his answer is favorable, I shall require every minute I can get to prepare myself to fill the position he has procured for me.

Your affectionate brother,
Stanley

———

10. Stanley's uncles, John Abbot and Ezra Abbot, were among the founders of Owatonna, Minnesota in 1855. Edwin hoped there might be a job for Stanley in the new town.

Newtonville, Massachusetts[11]
March 1, 1859

Dear Stanley,

Mr. Reid has just told me that you are absent from the store. . . . If you would keep the respect of those who know you, do be more faithful in your duties. I have gone back to my work relying upon your honor to keep your promise to me and your self-respect to make you faithful in giving to your employers the time which they have bought. If you would feel yourself an honest, not to say an honorable boy, you are bound to them and to me and to all the rest of your friends to keep your agreement. You engaged to me to stay at least a month, and you cannot honorably break your word.

I speak plainly. It is of the first importance to your reputation for more honesty to not avoid your duties at the store now for the short remaining time. I entreat you not to throw away now for so short an indulgence the regard of your employers, your own self-respect, and my respect for you as an honest truthful boy who, when he promises, keeps his promise however disagreeable it may be.

Once more I beg you to go back to your duties promptly and redeem your character as an honorable boy.

In haste yours affectionately,
Edwin

───眇───

Beverly
March 15, 1859

My dear Mary,

It has been a peaceful visit [at home with the family.] I came last night at six o'clock, and have had a long and more satisfactory talk than usual with Stanley. He is going to try and get some information about going to Exeter to

11. Home of Mary Carter who became Edwin's first wife on November 17, 1859 in spite of a terminal illness. She died three months later on February 17, 1860.

enter the Academy and [to make him] fit for College. I
rather tremble at the experiment and yet it is more his own
wish than anything else is. He is going to act himself. . . .
Last night I explained the matter to Stanley and told him
that I wanted him to act. Then I could only give him
advice profitably and help enlighten his understanding, but
that he ought to act, etc. And he, at length, assented and
seemed to understand that it was best. Now I shall only
advise and tell him what I think best. But he must form
his own plans and act at least in measure in trying to carry
them out. I do not know. I fear, but I will hope for the best.

> Goodbye, Yours always,
> Edwin

CHAPTER 4

A NEW LIFE

MAY, 1859–JUNE, 1860

What lies behind us and what lies before us are tiny matters
compared with what lies within us.

—UNKNOWN

Stanley decided on a college education after first considering
going to sea and a job out west with Uncle John. It is clear
from a later letter that he made this decision with the intent
of preparing himself to become a writer.[1] While Father Hale
had gone to Bowdoin, brothers Edwin and Frank had both
attended nearby Harvard, so that was the natural choice for
Stanley.[2]

There is no record of Stanley even considering other colleges. A year at a preparatory school was necessary to prepare
him for the entrance examination. Father Hale taught previously

---

1. See letter to Cousin Mattie from Stanley dated March 28, 1863 on
   page 189.
2. While proximity to Boston and Beverly was undoubtedly a prime
   reason for three of the four brothers attending Harvard, Hale may have
   urged Harvard partly to compensate for his own disappointment at
   not being able to go there. In a September 21, 1818 letter to his
   father, Ezra Abbot, Hale states: "On every account except expense I
   would much prefer to go to Cambridge rather than to Brunswick. . . .
   The expense [at Bowdoin] will be little more than half what it is at
   Cambridge."

EDWARD STANLEY ABBOT
SCHOOLBOY
circa 1859

at Phillips Exeter Academy, which was probably the reason
Stanley went there.[3]

>   Beverly
>   May 22, 1859
>
> Dear Edwin,
>   Mr. Bowen . . . says there will be no examination
> preparatory to entering the senior class at Exeter and
> he does not know exactly where the class will be at
> the beginning of the next term. . . . He says there is a
> scholarship or something of the sort which gives the room,
> tuition and $1.50 a week and, that if at the end of the
> 1st term I should stand high enough in the class to get the
> scholarship, they would pay it from the time I first entered
> the Academy.[4]
>
>   Your affectionate brother,
>   Stanley

Now that Stanley was leaving home for the first time, the
brothers flooded him with worldly advice that remains per-
tinent today. Edwin advised about how he should act and
react. Frank spoke about choosing and relating to friends.
Conspicuous in its absence was Father Hale's contribution. It
came nine months later—before Stanley started college—when
he advised his son on how and what to study.

>   North Conway
>   August 25, 1859
>
> My Dear Stanley,
>   You now cross the threshold of home, and go out from
> it into a new life which is all untried. Do not forget that it is
> meant only as a preparation for the fuller life of manhood
> in the world, and that it can be a happy life now only as
> you make it a faithful preparation for the succeeding life
> as a man. You come into new relations and with them new

---

3. Hale taught at Phillips Exeter from 1827 to 1833.
4. The $1.50 per week was apparently for meals.

duties. To specify them all would be neither possible nor useful. I can only give you a few unsatisfactory words of advice and brotherly counsel.

Do not forget the difference between home-confidence and school-intimacy. Others will really care for you in the exact ratio in which you, unselfishly and for their sakes, take an interest in them. Chumming, as I suppose you will have to chum, is a new experience.[5] It will try your temper and your principles and your judgment. You cannot be too kind and obliging, too ready to bear little annoyances cheerfully, and to make little sacrifices silently. You may make it a valuable experience and, even if you do not continue long together, there is no reason why you should not be friendly and part with kind feeling.

You will find it hard to rule your tongue wisely. Unkind words, harsh judgments, nicknames, wicked words, besides the host of idle words are constantly at hand and ready to rip out. They have to be watched, dear Stanley, and you will not have by you those who will be so willing to aid you as you have had and therefore your vigilance must be the greater.

In dealing with others, try to look at, to love, or to disapprove things not persons. Remember, evil is not unmixed any more than good in this world. Everyone has some good and that we should love and try to develop. Everyone has some evil and that we should not love and should try to put away. If in indiscriminate friendship or dislike we look at persons, rather than things in them, we shall certainly, be led wrong, and love or hate what is worthy of the reverse.

In your new position new evils will develop in yourself whose very existence you did not expect. Remember they come into view only that you may see them and put them away, and do not fail in the effort. We need never fail. It is our own fault if we do.

And now dear Stanley, good bye. You have with you love and all good wishes and many watch with loving

5. A chum was a roommate.

anxiety your going forth from home. I trust you or I should not have so furthered your plans. . . . May God bless you and guide your steps and give you His wisdom which passeth understanding.

> Affectionately, your brother,
> Edwin Hale Abbot

> Beverly
> September 7, 1859

Dear Stanley,

But I am sure that if you have not yet learned the meaning of the word "home-sick," it cannot be long before you do; and nothing is so good as a kind word of interest and affection from those at home when one's heart shrinks into itself from the cold, careless looks of strange faces.

But I want to say one word to you now when you are for the first time thrown among utter strangers. Do not shut yourself up in your room and think how miserable you are and how you long to go back to the old friends and places. Meet every little attention with a frank and grateful spirit and not despise it because it springs rather from a momentary good feeling than a long-tried friendship. This world is full of kindness if we will only open our eyes to it and nothing so wins friends to us as the manly desire to please all we have anything to do with, provided that desire is really a manly one.

I spoke to you one morning about choosing your companions wisely. I wish you could see how inexpressibly important this is. Your whole future course may depend on this single thing, and we all shall watch your progress with hope and love. Do not mistake the offhand jollity and good-nature of idle or thoughtless fellows for more than it is. Respond to it cordially but recollect that a valuable friendship is seldom of mushroom growth and cannot come at all from one who does not make duty his guiding principle of action.

A few years of experience will show you that I have underrated, rather than overrated, the importance of selecting large-hearted, brave, and faithful fellows for your friends in place of merely jolly, rich, and showy ones. Emmie and Katie both send lots of love and so does your aff. brother,

Frank

Stanley freely criticized the small town of Exeter, New Hampshire which offered far fewer opportunities than the Boston of Stanley's childhood or even the Beverly of his teenage years. But he enjoyed a visit with his mother's friend and a political rally.

Exeter
September 23, 1859

Dear [Sister] Emmie,

Exeter has been full of the "Rockingham Fair" and the men and things connected with it for the last week. Splendid placards were posted up all over the town announcing in huge capitals that there were to be numberless Military Companies and Bands present on the occasion, to say nothing of the Fair itself. Indeed so many were the notices stuck all over the houses and so great was the number of strange wagons continually passing through the town that at last I began to think that the Fair was going to be something worth seeing or at least that there would be a good many bumpkin militia companies to look at.

But alas their splendid 8 regiments or whatever they call them dwindled down into about a hundred Exeter braves who were obliged to borrow the uniform in which they paraded themselves. And before them marched the famous "Exeter Cornet Band" got up for the occasion likewise.

The whole thing reminded one of the fable of the ass in the lion's skin only in this case everybody was fox enough to know that their terrors were all borrowed, but nevertheless I venture to say that the above mentioned donkey did not occasion so much consternation by his fearful roar as our musical amateurs did by their hideous din. I never heard sounds so appalling and I never will again if it can be avoided.

Stanley

Exeter
October 25, 1859

Dear Edwin,

I have just returned from Mrs. Chadwick's where I have been making a call. She sent me word the other day through Mrs. Smith, who does my washing, that she wanted me to call on her as she knew my mother very well.[6] I saw no way of escape so I made up my mind to go on the first opportunity in order to get over a disagreeable job as quick as I could. I went and much to my astonishment I enjoyed myself. She is a nice old lady, full of all kind of stories, and she entertained me with at least a dozen in the hour I staid. I went there with the full intention of saying "good evening" as soon as I could with any sort of decency, but I was established so comfortably in an easy chair by the stove that I forgot all about it being a bore and staid more than an hour.

Your affectionate brother,
Stanley

Exeter
Christmas Eve, 1859

Dear [Sister] Emmie,

Don't you like to sit up Christmas Eve? I do not feel sleepy a bit. There is almost a fascination in it for me. I don't know when I shall go to bed. I had much rather draw the table up to the fire and talk to my dear sister away off in Boston. . . . Did you never feel as if you were as old as

---

6. Fanny and Hale lived in Exeter from their marriage in 1830 until 1833.

the hills? Sometimes it seems perfectly frightful the idea of living to grow old. I wonder how many more Christmas Eves I shall sit up to write letters and to hear the solemn old bell toll out twelve as it did just now. The house is all still and the fire is cracking away in the stove so as to remind me of the "cricket on the hearth." Is there not something very cheerful in a wood fire? Sometimes I think there is and then it seems as mournful as the tolling of the bell.

Your affectionate brother,
Stanley

STANLEY'S JOURNAL

February 1, 1860. I think I will begin a journal. I shall find it a relief to have somebody to whom I can say what I will—someone who will not misunderstand me, who will never wrong me, and whom I can never wrong. I will personify this book. I will have a friend to whom I can be unreserved. I wonder if I am different from everybody else. Sometimes it seems as if I were. I have thoughts and feelings which I do not see in others—tonight I have had a "quarrel," as most persons would call it, with my chum. He is very conceited, very hypocritical, or very weak. I cannot tell exactly which. I have tried to love him and I cannot. I have been disappointed. I do not think I can love anybody.

February 15, 1860. I have not paid you any very marked attention lately, have I—but what is your name? Here I have been making an ideal friend for myself and have not even given him a name to distinguish him from other people! What shall I call you? I will call you "friend." That will forever belong to you alone! No fear of confounding you with others, as long as I shall live. I shall hardly find another on whom I can bestow that title. But I was making my excuses to you, friend, for not having chatted with you for so long—but why should I apologize to you?

You speak to me as my double. A mirror, you show me myself. Are you then a friend? I fear not. Those who are truly friendly to themselves always have others to love them. "To him that hath shall be given, but from him that hath not shall be taken away even that little which he hath. . . ."

The older I grow the more impossible it seems to me to open myself to anybody. I cannot talk to Mother or Emmie, much less to Edwin, of what I really feel. It seems as if it were absolutely impossible for me to make a confidante of anyone and yet I know very well . . . that true friendship cannot exist without perfect confidence. It is this knowledge of my own secretiveness that makes me sure I shall never have a *Fidus Achates.*[7]

Stanley was not alone in attending Phillips Exeter for a year in order to prepare for the entrance examinations to Harvard. Abraham Lincoln wished for his eldest son, Robert Todd Lincoln, the formal education that he lacked. But Robert failed the Harvard entrance examinations in 1859, so he too attended Phillips Exeter the same year as Stanley in order to prepare for his next attempt at gaining admission. Both entered the freshman class at Harvard in the fall of 1860.[8]

At the end of February, Lincoln—at that time a presidential aspirant—took advantage of an invitation to speak in New York City to visit Robert at his prep school, and to speak in various cities throughout New England. His speech at the Exeter Town Hall[9] came only a few days after his famous Cooper Union speech in New York City on February 27, and he reiterated many of the same themes there.[10]

---

7. A *Fidus Achates* is an intimate companion. The literal translation is "good, faithful Achates." Achates was such a friend to Aeneas in Virgil's *Aeneid,* a Latin epic poem. http://en.wikipedia.org/wiki/Achates. Last updated July 24, 2011.

8. http://en.wikipedia.org/wiki/Robert_Todd_Lincoln. Last updated October 2, 2011.

9. http://www.seacoastonline.com/articles/20090125-NEWS-901250339.

10. http://www.abrahamlincolnsclassroom.org/Library/newsletter.asp?ID=41&CRLI=121.

It is likely that Stanley and/or Edwin knew Robert Lincoln. However, no reference to him is found in Stanley's or Edwin's papers.

Exeter
March 4, 1860

Dear Mother,

Exeter is such a dull old hole that a week here is equal to a year anywhere else. To be sure lately it has not been quite so still as usual for the Republicans have opened the Presidential campaign by holding a "Grand Rally" in the Town Hall. The famous "Abe Lincoln," the man who canvassed Illinois against Douglas, addressed the patriotic "opposition" of ye Goody town of Exeter, ditto Mr. Underwood of Virg[inia]. Lincoln is one of those long, lean, liberty-pole looking sort of men that are always so awkward and usually so "smart."[11] He gave the best st[ump] speech I ever heard. It was capital. He has a good deal of dramatic hours and he does not display it too much so as to disgust one. Everyone knows how bitterly opposed he is to his rival Douglas and it was splendid fun to see him lay it on to Douglas thick and thin. He seemed to take such pleasure in it.

From your loving son,
Stanley

STANLEY'S JOURNAL

April 11, 1860. I have just got back from my vacation. I have had a reasonably good time. Of course, I did not enjoy myself as much as I expected to but yet I have no reason to complain. I am glad my stay in Exeter will be so short. I

---

11. "A liberty pole is a tall wooden pole, often used as a type of flagstaff, planted in the ground, which may be surmounted by an ensign or a liberty cap." http://en.wikipedia.org/wiki/liberty pole. Last updated April 23, 2012.

am sick to death of it and everything in it and I can't help looking forward to college with anticipation of enjoyment. I suppose when I get there I shall be impatient to get out and so on all my life though always looking forward with impatience.

Exeter
April 22, 1860

Dear [Sister] Emmie,

I meant to have written to you long ago and I should have carried out my intention if I had not followed your advice about the May flowers. One day I went out into the woods and got some of them and since that time I have been wildflower mad. I have been out time, time and again until my room is full of them and the whole atmosphere of the room is at this moment heavy with their scent. I never was so taken off my feet in my life by anything as I have been by these little flowers. You would laugh if you could hear all the fine plans I have laid of studying botany and having hot houses and conservatories and model farms etc. etc. "when I am a rich man." But the disease is leaving me and I have come to the conclusion that I can enjoy God's flowers in God's conservatory fully as well as I could in a glass one belonging to Edward Stanley Abbot.

"It never rains but it pours." There never was a truer saying uttered on this earth than this. Not only have I become enamored of May flowers but I set off one afternoon in a rain storm to get some evergreens to decorate our room! I got two different kinds and I made wreaths and hung long streamers all over my pictures and bookshelves until I really began to think I had a very decided taste in adorning rooms. Indeed so imbued was I in this belief that I went to bed in the firm belief that I was an artist!

But, oh horror! In the morning when I awoke I found that the little sprigs I had arranged with so much care and trouble had all shrunk out of place. The wreaths were no longer round and in fact the whole concern looked decidedly shabby. It was considerable of a "come down" but still I was not disheartened and, though I could not restore the original appearance, I still succeeded in making them look quite respectable.

> So goodbye with ever
> so much love,
> from Stanley

Boston
May 4, 1860

Dear Stanley,

Recollect that next to virtuous Christian character, a sound comprehensive judgment is the great thing to be aimed at your period of life, as "the last product of the finished understanding" and that it can be attained only by a patient, thorough discipline of the intellectual faculties and the formations of good intellectual habits.

A superficial survey of a wide field of reading for study profits but little while the careful, thorough, profound examination and mastery of one single subject is productive of great, very great, benefit.[12] I hope you will practice daily on some passage for improving your habits of speech and acquiring a clear, distinct, and deliberate utterance.

Even if you do not appreciate the importance of it as I do, trust to my advice now. You will defy our lives at some future time. See that the advice is wise and regret most deeply any neglect to follow it on your part.

> Yours affectionately,
> Jos. Hale Abbot

---

12. Hale himself did master more than one subject. He not only developed a new method of teaching English grammar, but also gave lectures at the Boston Athenæum on scientific subjects.

Exeter

May 13, 1860

Dear [Sister] Emmie,

I meant to have written to you before but you know I have always been famous for breaking good resolutions and therefore it is not to be wondered at that I have failed in this respect and still less is it to be regretted by you. I believe I shall never conquer my aversion to letter writing. It is inborn and therefore unconquerable but there is one comfort connected with this conviction of mine, i.e. that by yielding to the natural instinct I shall gratify my friends no less than myself.

Your loving Stanley

Exeter

June 30, 1860

Dear Edwin,

You spoke of my coming to Cambridge Saturday before examination. My plan was to walk over to Salem Monday morning and take the first train for Boston. I shall feel nervous enough under any circumstances and, I confess, I fairly dread being at the scene of suffering so long before the execution. I expect to be utterly miserable until I have "saved my bacon" or "broken my nose" (as Exeter boys call entering without or with conditions) but it would be unnecessary torture it seems to me to spend my last hour in sight of the guillotine and to have my last Sunday at the disposal of one of the executioners![13] To tell the truth, I feel very uncomfortable as the trial draws near. I think I ought to get in all straight and yet I firmly believe I shall be conditioned. Altogether I should make a very bad companion for you and I don't think I could go to church to any benefit at all on that day. I never read any description of the misery of anticipation that comes up to the reality!

Your loving brother,

Stanley

---

13. Edwin must have proctored the examination.

---◦◦◦---

CHAPTER 5

A NEW WORLD
SEPTEMBER, 1860–MARCH, 1861

A University should be a place of light, of liberty, and of learning.
—BENJAMIN DISRAELI

Stanley did satisfactorily on the exams. On July 17, 1860, he entered Harvard "on probation" as did all students during their first year in that era.

> Cambridge
> September [n.d.], 1860

Dear [Sister] Emmie,

Everything goes on much as usual. I am getting more and more into the habit of college duties and I like them more and more. I shudder when I think of India Street and that I might very likely have been there still if I had not been a naughty boy and rebelled against the powers that be, taken the bit between my teeth, and made a declaration of independence on a small scale.[1] I can't see the evil effects of my obstinacy, I confess.

> Stanley

---

1. India Street is a reference to the location of Reed, Cutler & Co., the wholesale druggist where Stanley worked before attending Phillips Exeter Academy.

49

As a typical freshman, Stanley quickly realized that he left a few things at home.

> Cambridge
> September 8, 1860

Dear Mother,

I don't know as my date is right. . . . Alas! The injury received by my patience is, I fear, nearly if not quite fatal. You know it always was in very delicate health and unable to bear severe shocks. Now, I am sorry to inform you, it is in the last stages of consumption. Indeed it is, to speak more correctly, wholly consumed and I don't know where to look for its substitute. Words fail me when I attempt to make them convey to you an adequate conception of the sickening longing I have had and have for that most important article of furniture.

Never lover longed for mistress as I for my washstand. I have refrained from making visits to other rooms for fear I should catch a glimpse of a pitcher and the casual view of a basin the other day threw me into despair deeper than any well. However, I will write no more on this most melancholy subject though, were I inclined, I might fill reams about it and use as ink the tears I have shed darkened by the dirt I have been unable to wash from my face and hands.

I received the shoes with great thankfulness. They somewhat consoled for my great sorrow. . . . The following is a list of the things I want.

1. One pillow (a soft one preferred).

2. The piece of carpet I had at Exeter for bedroom.

3. The pair of buff, thin pants now at home.

4. The little glass lamp brought from Exeter.

5. The "leather-flower picture frame" Emmy gave me and which I forgot to bring with me.

6. My suspenders, forgotten, with most disastrous consequences. . . .

7. Please ask Emmie to look among my pictures and see if she can find two that will fit the two largest frames I brought with me. She can tell the size by the one I left at Beverly. Also, can she let me have the two pictures she promised to draw for me, now? If so please send all four with the box and also the pen drawing if, as I am afraid is unlikely, she does not want it for a show "picture."

8. Because, since for the reason that and whereas I love cookies, if so be as how, as if you can, without inconvenience send me a few I shall be duly grateful.

That is about all I want I believe and if you could send these by Grout in the course of a week or so or whenever it is convenient for you I shall be the most grateful of human beings. . . .

Well! I declare, as Leafy Patch (Is that spelt right? By the way, what is that person's real name?) used to say "when I sat down to write this I honestly intended to give an account of myself and my doings good boy fashion" but I have got over the ground somehow and have not begun so yet; so I may as well give it up and wait till next time which will be exactly a week from this date for, I would have you know, I intend to be the very best of correspondents and to write you a letter every Sunday with the regularity of clockwork. . . .

Please give love to Emmie and tell her to WRITE, also to Willie, and with ever so much to yourself, I am

Your loving son,
Stanley

FRANCIS ELLINGWOOD ABBOT
1836–1903

Stanley's prior journal had its last entry on April 11, 1860. Frank encouraged him to start one again.

STANLEY'S JOURNAL

College Life
As it appears to
Edward Stanley Abbot
Being a record of the
Deeds and Misdeeds,
Haps and Mishaps
Of that individual while a student
At the
University of Cambridge.
Vol. I

Cambridge, September 14, 1860. My Brother Frank came to see me the other day, and after talking about various things for some time, he suddenly turned round and said, in the quick way of one who has just received a smart blow from an idea, "By the way Stan, do you keep a journal?" I informed him that I did not and gave as my reason that diaries and journals were usually, as I thought, the most egotistical of those painfully egotistical productions given birth to in such profusion by young gentlemen and young ladies (Heaven forbid I should slight "the Ladies. God bless 'em") "of a certain age."

He replied that was all true enough, "But," said he, "if you fail to keep an account of your college course, you will find that you will forget many pleasant things, of no great importance perhaps, but still things you will be glad to think over when college life has long been past and you begin to take in retrospection no small proportion of the happiness which now you look for in the future alone."

It struck me there might be a good deal of truth in this and I, on consideration, came to the conclusion that the egotism, which will appear in these pages, would do me no very serious damage, while at some future day to look back upon the thoughts and hopes, the loves and hates, the sorrows and the joys of earlier, and probably happier years, might give me pleasure. So, since I am a confirmed voluptuary, the upshot of the matter was that I went to the expense of 42 cents in purchasing a Blank Book. To be filled up how?

May I have no reason to say when its pages are filled "I wish I were 42 cents richer. I wish I had never bought this book or, having bought it, had never stained its purity with the record of my life." I have another "blank book" to fill whose leaves are yet as pure as these. God grant that when my hairs are grey, and its leaves are also full, I may have no reason to say: "Would they were unwritten. Would my story had ended where it was begun?" I have an old journal and an old life. I am glad they are ended, and that I have once more a starting point. For I seem to myself to begin over again in a new world, under different circumstances, with different aims than I ever had before.

———

Cambridge
September 16, 1860

Dear Mother,

Here it is Sunday once more and I have just got back from breakfast and am going to write to you the first thing I do. This week has passed very swiftly. The wheels are getting well-greased so that they run easily and I feel actually settled at last. N. B., one great reason of my feeling so, I take to be, that the washstand HAS come.

To be sure it is in a very dilapidated condition. The top being entirely wrenched off and part of the crockery smashed. I was not at my room when it was brought and the express man left it in front of my door exposed to the operations of some sophs who are on the same floor with myself. I suppose I owe these gentlemen the favor of my broken crockery and smashed washstand. I hope they enjoyed their haze!

I am getting into a regular routine which does not vary much from day to day and, in the course of a week or two more, I hope to be a naturalized student. At twenty five minutes after six every morning the first bell for prayers rings and at quarter of seven exactly I take my seat in the chapel just before the second bell ceases to toll. First, Mr. Peabody reads a chapter from the Bible, then the choir sings a chant or something of the sort followed by a prayer of the Dr.'s, and that business is done.

Right after prayers I go to get my breakfast (at Mrs. Wyeth's. At first I boarded at the Brattle but soon got disgusted with the filth and left.) After breakfast I go back to my room, look over my morning lesson, and at eight go in to recite it. Next recitation comes at eleven and the third and last at four in the afternoon. From eight till five I am occupied either in getting or reciting my lessons but all the rest of the time I have to myself for we get such short lessons that I always get my evening lesson in the afternoon. So you see I am not likely "to lose my health from a too unwearied application." I had to study a great deal harder at Exeter than I do now. . . .

There goes the first bell for church and I have got lots of things to do before the second rings, so I must shorten this letter. . . .

Give Willie a kiss for me and tell him he may congratulate himself on its coming through a letter for if I administered it in person, it would probably be metamorphosed into a smack.

Your affectionate son,
Stanley

Cambridge
September 29, 1860

Dear Mother,

I am getting along in a very monotonous and pleasant way and I enjoy myself very much. . . . I cannot be

sufficiently glad that I did not stay at Exeter another
year. To be sure now that Frank is gone it is not nearly as
pleasant but still it is near Boston which I always have
regarded and always shall regard as my real home.[2] I
am getting acquainted with my classmates and though I
have not fallen in love with any of them, still I find them a
"pretty clever set" take them all in all.

Love to all from Stanley

Edwin supported Stanley financially from the time Stanley
went away to Phillips Exeter until he finally began earning a
living in the Army. Lengthy reports of expenses exist to document the pre-approval and accounting that Edwin demanded
from Stanley in return for financial support. From time to time
Stanley rebelled from this control as might any teenager. A later
letter to Henry from his wife, Susie, explained the situation.[3]

Cambridge
August 29, 1861

Dear Henry,
    Although I respect and love Edwin as a warm-hearted
and high principled man, yet I think it would be a very
annoying thing to have to receive money through him. I
think with all his excellence, he does love to control others
and manage their affairs, do you not? . . . If Stanley had
a certain sum allowed him he could contrive to keep his
expenses down to that allowance and not have his pride
grated upon by the necessity of going to Edwin to have
small sums doled out."

Susie

Stanley's teenage rebellion let loose as open warfare broke
out between Stanley and Edwin toward the end of 1860. It

---

2. Frank left Harvard earlier in September to attend the seminary in
   Meadville, Pennsylvania.
3. Catherine C. Abbot, *Family Letters of General Henry Larcom Abbot,
   1831–1927* (Gettysburg: Thomas Publications, 2001), 45.

EDWIN HALE ABBOT
1834–1927

is interesting to note that the two brothers, who both lived on the Harvard campus at the time, chose to write letters to each other on October 30, 1860, rather than speak face-to-face. It is not clear whether one letter was written on receipt of the other, or they were written independently and crossed in the mail. What is clear is that the tension between the two was great at this point in their relationship. The two letters follow.

Cambridge
October 30, 1860

Dear Edwin,

I have not written before for several reasons. One of which reasons was that you might know by the time that has passed that I have no unkindly feelings about what was the immediate cause of our—what shall I call it?—quarrel. . . . I agree with you in thinking that our intercourse for the last five years has been a false one and I, as well as you, desire to place it upon a new and a true footing.

From earliest childhood, as far as my memory goes back, until the present moment your influence has been incomparably more powerful over me than that of any other human being. That influence will continue to be incomparably superior to that of any other till the day of my death. I wish it to be so, I am conscious it will be so.

When I entered Mr. Dixwell's [Latin] school, the peculiar relations we sustained to one another vastly increased your power over me. I was at that time a mere child in age, in intellect, in experience, in will. . . . Your opinion was mine on all subjects. . . . I grew older and began to think for myself.

I could not see all things as you saw them. I differed from you on many things, but the habit of deference to your opinion held me like a vice.

I took refuge in silence. I wish you clearly to understand that the struggle for freedom was not with you. It was with myself, and when I pained you, as I often did by showing what you thought a dogged disposition to reject your advice on all matters, I in reality was so utterly miserable in resisting you that, when I spoke to you most sharply and cruelly, I longed most to throw my arms round your neck and cry for your forgiveness.

Edwin, you understand me and you don't understand. In some things you utterly misconceive my character. . . . I don't want to reject your love nor your advice. I want both, but I do want to free my own love for you from the servility and the cowardice that has marked it heretofore. It is inexpressibly painful to me to have our money relations as they are, and I honestly and coolly say I think it would be best for both of us to have them discontinued.

I am more of a man than you think me. The bonds between you and me, which five years ago were right and proper, are no longer such. I ask you to recognize the difference five years has made in me. You tell me to assign the limits of our intercourse. Let them be those of closest friendship.

I wish you to know that, if we are to be friends and brothers, we cannot have between us any such relation as that about money. The only reason you give for it is that it will draw us closer together—it has been the thing which has parted us.

Stanley

Cambridge
October 30, 1860

My dear boy,

I write you a few words which I wish to have you think of kindly and wisely, and which I earnestly wish to separate from any harsh or unpleasant sound or thought. Fancy yourself at Exeter again and let me have the old brotherly freedom once more.

I want to have you free, really truly free, most of all free from selfishness and wrong. To accomplish this I am ready to do anything which you choose to decide. . . .

I want to propose to you what may lessen a natural embarrassment in this, your new position, and for the last time to give you advice which is unsought.

My proposition is this. Any new pecuniary arrangement which you desire to make is not very easily made and will probably require a good deal of time and thought. Until that is satisfactorily made (and do not rashly precipitate it, until you fully understand it), come to me for all the money you need without hesitation and you shall have the required sums without delay (if possible) and certainly without question or interference.

You shall be your own master and, as far as I am concerned, the sole judge of the necessity which calls for it.

If you wish advice or counsel on any subject, you can give me no greater pleasure in life than to come to me as your brother, and I will try to receive you as you come. But henceforth and forever let all unkind words, looks, tones, all innuendoes and sarcasms, everything in short but personal kindness of manner and feeling disappear between us.

To me, it seems clear that as long as you are borrowing money, it is wrong to indulge in little superfluities which are harmless to others perhaps and which it is natural to desire. A debt is a sacred thing and every cent obtained by increasing debt is rigidly to be accounted for in the light of a true conscience.

You are now going to assume a great responsibility. You claim full freedom and to be your own master. Do not forget that the Lord is the master of us all, or to seek his counsel through His word. Do not forget also that it is a test of wisdom to let the experience of others stand for our own and save us from their errors.

Your brother,
Edwin

Cambridge
November 10, 1860

Dear Stanley,

I have not yet had an answer to the letter I wrote you and I am waiting uneasily for it.

For the same reason that I wrote to you, I want you to sit down and in a kindly brotherly way write to me as much of your plans as you choose, but at any rate exactly what you want me to do and not to do. I am sure you will see the reasonableness and the necessity of this, at least to me who am expected to act and am entirely ready and glad to act when I know just how. . . .

But after what you have told me of the effect of my trying to help you in my way, I do not dare for your own good to do anything more than you ask me to do. . . .

As matters now stand the old intercourse is all gone, and you have not yet given me a plan of the need. I can hardly believe that you feel satisfied with our present brotherly relations. . . . I do not say it unkindly (you know I do not) but I feel so completely thrown off by your declarations, that I am determined not to make similar mistakes again. I give it all into your hands. So far as you will invite me to draw near and come into brotherly confidence and counsel, I shall love indeed to come.

But I cannot, after what you have said and done (and because I myself think there is truth in much of what you said), go one hair's breadth farther than you invite me. If from this time our paths divide and the old confidence between us dies into more external friendliness, it will be the most painful thing in life, but it must be, unless you yourself choose to have it otherwise.

And so I want you to calmly and wisely and thoughtfully and kindly write me in all our relations what you desire. Please be careful in what you say for I shall follow it, as far as I think I can rightly, to the letter. We have duties to one another, I to you and you to me.

Affectionately, your brother,
Edwin

Cambridge
November 12, 1860

My dear Stanley,

Your letter gives me great pleasure. I want to do just what you say in it. Let our intercourse be that of "closest friendship" between two men which it will every day tend to become.[4] I only want you to live in subjection to truth, not at all to me, and I will try to help you only in your efforts to see and to live that truth. Still we must both watch ourselves. You must ask and seek more and I must volunteer less. That's what I mean by your setting the limit. . . .

I want you though to see clearly that you must do a great deal more than you ever have done in seeking that friendship and confidential intercourse. . . .

I must be careful in what I do, and you must come out of yourself toward me more than you ever have done. I hope you will come to feel that whenever you are in trouble or temptation, you will wish to come to me for comfort and counsel and without any fear of being enslaved. Whatever influence is real, comes always from the truth, for truth alone has and uses the power of love.

With love,
Edwin

STANLEY'S JOURNAL

December 19, 1860. I wonder if it is of any use for me to keep this journal. I seldom write in it. That is sure. However, I will try to do better in the future. How fortunate it is that we live in the future so entirely because that is all our own. It is only the present and the past over which we have no control. . . .

4. See letter to Edwin from Stanley dated October 30, 1860 on page 58 in which he states, "You tell me to assign the limits of our intercourse. Let them be those of closest friendship."

College and college life. What of it? Well, I like it, and I don't like it. . . .

How little we really know. Men pride themselves upon wisdom. How profitless the knowledge which is found in the consciousness of ignorance! And yet that is the only thing the wisest of mortals have taught us. They say that is as far as wisdom can go! Ought we not to go back to childish folly rather than press on so earnestly in the pursuit of that which all men strive for, wisdom, when the wisest man said before he died "vanity of vanities, all is vanity."

If truth be infinitely good and pure how can we, finite as we are, approximate after all our struggles to the infinite? Are not all our thoughts and yearnings, tears and sorrows, and disappointments the miserable silliness of children crying for the moon? Why not live in the present, enjoy the heat of the fire, the food we eat, the indulgencies we can procure for ourselves. . . .

Why should God be love when his creatures whom he made even in his own image are often incarnate hate? I suffer. Is not infinite power capable to end that suffering? Is not infinite love kind enough to seek to do so? How strange that we, who are finite in all things else, should seek to grasp the infinite in time. . . .

I shall struggle into life once more, a flower perhaps, and perhaps the very hand which pens these lines unnumbered ages hence may once more be a hand which shall pen other lines, as hopeless and as blind as these. "And so we go, bobbing around, around." Who knows what is to be? Not I. I have but one hope, one prayer. May no atom that makes me be ever again part or parcel of sentient being! Take from me the Tantalus gift of thought!

———

Meadville
February 19, 1861

Dear Stanley,

As my vacation has come now, I will fulfill my promise of answering your letter. . . .

I cannot but feel a little alarmed at what you write about your relations with Edwin. However, I hope all will turn out well. But you will find more difficulty in getting money than you anticipate. It comes hard and goes quick. You do not say anything about your prospect of a scholarship. I do hope you will not miss that. It is worth digging for, night and day.

If you ever do get hard up and can't see your way out of a corner, just send me word, and I will do all I can. This year I am pinched myself, or I would not wait to be asked. I feel the greatest sympathy for you, for I know it is a wretched piece of business to be borrowing money; better scrimp and play the miser over every copper than owe another for it. If you can only get a scholarship, all will go straight; otherwise you will get deep in debt; and debt is a hair shirt to your back. . . .

I wish much I could be with you in Cambridge. There is no use in denying it. There is great danger, moral and pecuniary, to a young man thrown upon himself in the midst of college society. I thought that if I could have stayed with you, I should have had your confidence, and might have helped you over some quagmires and rough places in your college course. But coming away as I did, I feel more than a brother's interest and anxiety for your welfare. Now do write me about the important things, like a dear fellow as you are, and not leave me in ignorance of what is really happening to you. You need not fear that what you write will leak out through me. Show me the confidence you know I deserve and make me your friend. "Blood is thicker than water." Brothers do not grow on every bush.

Your brother,
Frank E. A.

Dover
February 22, 1861

Dear Stanley,

If you desire it, as I understand you do, I am ready to do all I can and we will start at least in the Term as you proposed last January.[5] I do not see any reason why all should not go well and why you may not learn much and save much by the arrangement. Of course, you understand that the scholarship is assigned to pay the debts of the past year and so when you receive and what you receive from such college sources will be used to pay the debts of the past year. I fear that I cannot find the money under any other arrangement, for I am very short and shall have to use my own credit to borrow it now.

Love to all,
Edwin

At Harvard, Stanley did not concentrate solely on his studies, which occasioned some discord between him and Edwin. In a published memorial to his brother, Edwin notes:

He practically trained himself for an author's work, as is shown by a little incident of which he told me in almost the last conversation we ever had. While he was in the Freshman year, a former friend had fallen into temptation, and embezzled fifty dollars from his employer. In despair, he told Stanley. Stanley at once, without saying anything of his design, wrote some stories, sold them, got the fifty dollars, and gave them to the boy. He mentioned this casually to me as a piece of Quixotry, which had caused some neglect in his college duties, for which I had blamed him at the time.[6]

In spite of Edwin's promise "to come to me for all the money you need without hesitation and you shall have the required sums without delay (if possible) and certainly without

---

5. A January letter has not been found. Perhaps this proposal was made face-to-face.
6. Edwin H. Abbot, "Edward Stanley Abbot," in *Harvard Memorial Biographies*, ed. Thomas Higginson, vol. II (Cambridge: Sever and Francis, 1866), 432. Where the stories were published is unknown. There are no copies in Stanley's files.

question or interference," Stanley remained uncomfortable in seeking funds from Edwin.[7]

> Cambridge
> March 24, 1861

Dear Mother,

I have no particular news to write about. All goes on the old jog trot that is usual in term time. The studies are regular and interesting especially in Latin. We are reading Horace and I like him ever so much. He has more genius a thousand fold than that dull, prosy old codger of a Virgil, who was always most confoundedly uninteresting to me. . . .

My chum and I get along admirably together. I think I was very fortunate in getting so good a fellow for roommate. I was very glad indeed to get your letter and Em's and I am sorry I could not answer them before but, really, it is a most galling thing to get money from Ed and I did without a cent for weeks rather than ask him.

> Yr. loving son,
> Stanley

7. See letter to Stanley from Edwin dated October 30, 1860 on page 59.

CHAPTER 6

SACRILEGIOUS, FRIGHTFUL, CAUSELESS WAR
APRIL, 1861–JUNE, 1861

North and South they assembled, one cry and the other cry,
And both are ghosts to us now, old drums hung up on a wall,
But they were the first hot wave of youth too-ready to die,
And they went to war with an air, as if they went to a ball.
—STEPHEN VINCENT BENÉT, *John Brown's Body*

Rumors of war filled the land in the spring of 1861. Less than two weeks before the attack on Fort Sumter, Stanley expressed strong feelings of patriotism.

STANLEY'S JOURNAL

April 4, 1861. Before the opera began the orchestra played "Hail Columbia," and Miss Hinckley sang "The Star Spangled Banner," holding the American flag.[1] She did it beautifully and was encored. I declare I felt a sensation of patriotism when I saw the beauty stand there in the blazing light, waving the grand old national standard. The tears actually started to my eyes when I thought of what

---

1. Isabella Hinckley sang the part of Princess Eugenia in the opera *La Juive* by Fromental Halevy at the Academy of Music on April 1. This is probably the performance to which Stanley refers. Advertisement, *Boston Daily Advisor*, April 1, 1861.

a glory and of what a disgrace that bit of colored silk and the emblem. It is easy to learn love of country when the lesson is taught by a graceful singer and a lovely woman. How much our virtue has to do with accident and external influences! Because Miss Hinckley sang most charmingly a noble song, I and 3000 people beside felt the love of our nationland rise warm in our hearts.

Perhaps there ought to be as much of pathos in the newspaper telegram, when one reads there of the ruin of this country, but the tears come only when the eye and the ear give to the dormant feeling of sorrow life and expression. . . .

The opera, which followed the National Anthem, was magnificent and was said to be much the best rendered of the season.

One seems to live an age in the course of an opera. The excitement is absolutely intoxicating to me and it is so hard to leave the fairyland of harmony and come down to actual plain matter of fact life that we understand why Mirabeau whispered with his last breath "Cover me with roses. Let me die to the sound of delicious music." Anything but music seems disgusting after music. Cadmus did not invent so much of a wonder after all for letters cannot paint feeling but only thought, and feeling rules not only the world but the best and wisest of the *tout le monde*.

Shortly after Stanley and Edwin reconciled, the country came apart at the Battle of Fort Sumter on April 12–13, 1861. Stanley was profoundly affected.

STANLEY'S JOURNAL

April 14, 1861. Today everyone is in a fever about Fort Sumter. Yesterday it was said that the Fort had been taken and Major Anderson captured. Now the report is that the

Federal army has landed, stormed . . . Cumming's Point especially. . . . Great news, if true. I only hope it is. I am against the war but if it must come, in God's name let us have no baby work at the outset. Let the struggle be bloody, decisive and short.

Now that the war is here one feels heart sick. The glory of the country seems ended and who can fathom the depth of misery into which it may be plunged? Ah! It is a sacrilegious, frightful, causeless war!

What must be the verdict of posterity upon our abolitionists? They have shattered the fabric it cost so many agonies, such tears, such blood to rear and cement. They may be honest but they are pitiful blunderers, these republicans. They have neither the courage to follow their axiom to its logical results and side with that honest and courageous fanatic Wendell Phillips[2] nor have they sagacity to lay hold of the only American principle, "Squatter Sovereignty," and call Douglas their leader.[3] Well, not only they and we, but the millions of wretches who shall constitute our successors may weep tears of blood over their cowardly fanaticism!

What shall be the end of all this? *Quien sabe?* I cannot feel other than glad that the glorious old Star Spangled Banner shall not sink without a gallant struggle. I cannot help feeling proud and happy if it has floated once more over a field of victory when it followed the bayonets that swept the accursed rebels from Cumming's Point and won back Fort Moultrie to the North. We may not kill Secession but it shall writhe and lick the dust for all that!

April 19, 1861. MacElrath came in. Poor fellow he told us he is going tomorrow at 8. He got leave of absence

---

2. A Massachusetts abolitionist.

3. "The doctrine of 'Squatter Sovereignty' was based on the theory that the people of any state or territory should have the right to regulate their domestic institutions as they might see fit, particularly the institution of slavery." Frank Blackmar, ed., *Kansas: A Cyclopedia of State History* (Chicago: Standard Publishing Company, 1912), vol. II, 732.

from the Pres. today and is off for the South.[4] He feels
sadly about going, and it was as much as he could do
to keep from bursting into tears several times. We talked
about the war, not in argument, but as sheer regret led us
to speak, and sad enough we felt! Mac and I have been
good friends. Many a pleasant evening I have passed with
him. Many a game of chess have I played with him, and
many a time I have thought I liked him as well as any in
the class.

Well, we have parted never to meet again or perhaps
to meet in battle. Who can tell where this frightful quarrel
will lead us? I may be drafted, and he is sure to join the
Confederate Army, and who can say we may not meet
hereafter as mortal foes who in the old times held each
other so fondly?

Poor fellow, he wished to see Edwin ever so much,
for he fitted Mac for college, and always treated him right
kindly, and Mac says he will be round to see Edwin in the
morning before prayers.[5] He nearly cried when he said he
could never be back here again. "For if you whip us," said
he, "as you will, for you are the biggest, no Southern man
will ever plant his foot on Northern soil." He tried hard to
conceal his feelings but he could not, and as he stood in
the doorway, grasping my hand so cordially and strongly
his voice shook, and I saw the tears falling down his cheeks
when he said "write to me, old fellow, and I will answer
you, honour bright, secession or no secession, and there's
my hand upon it," giving me an honest grip, and then he
walked sadly away in the darkness, and I shall see him no
more this side of the grave.

---

4. The Harvard president at the time was Cornelius Conway Felton. It
is interesting that a leave of absence was granted by the president of
Harvard to a student to fight for the South. MacElrath did not return
to Harvard after the war. It is noteworthy that only the deaths of
northern soldiers were commemorated in Harvard's Memorial Hall
built after the Civil War. One wonders if Mac would have been welcome if he had tried to return to Harvard from his leave of absence.

5. Edwin must have tutored Mac for the Harvard entrance exams.

My God! What a frightful thing this horrible war is! Oh we do not see it when the blood within us boils high, and blind sectional enthusiasm makes fratricides of us all in heart! But sometimes there must be pauses in the tragedy between the acts, and then its appalling bitterness sweeps down and crushes us. Oh how America will weep in tears of bitter agony and oceans of blood the blindness that has fallen upon us like a curse from the Almighty!

It will be a war of opinion and principle, for both sides honestly believe they are doing God good service. Who shall tell the end? What an end to the gorgeous drama of the American Republic, civil war, anarchy, and looming darkly in the dim and gloomy future, military despotism! 86 years ago today was fought the first good fight of the Revolution and this day has seen the opening act of the tragedy in the streets of Baltimore.[6] The first blood has been drawn in a land conflict. The union is crumbling. Ere yet it has survived the paltry century its opponents ever granted for its life! The ways of the God of hosts are inscrutable and in his hand are the destinies of this ruined land.

In a letter to his mother on the same day Stanley added additional details of the leave-taking.

Cambridge
April 19, 1861

Dear Mother,

MacElrath, a Southerner, has just left the room; he came to bid me goodbye for he is going to the South and doubtless he will join the Confederate army. He is as good a fellow as ever breathed and he cried like a baby when he bade me goodbye. He and I have been right good friends and I cannot well tell what a pang I felt to see him walk

---

6. "When the Sixth Massachusetts Regiment reached Baltimore by rail en route to defend Washington, the men were attacked by a secessionist mob. . . . Four soldiers and nine civilians were killed." Doris Kearns Goodwin, *Team of Rivals: The Political Genius of Abraham Lincoln* (New York: Simon & Schuster, 2005), 352.

off into the darkness and hear him sob as he walked. I will never see him again this side of the grave.

He told me poor fellow, "Abbot, you will thrash us to pieces. You have all the power, but God knows it shall not be without a struggle! No one loved the union more than I and you cannot know what it will cost me to raise my arm against the stars and stripes but God has willed it and God's will be done! Write to me before the mails are closed and I will write back secession or no secession!" 'Tis a horrible war that is upon us! And everyone seems so blind, the streets are full of enthusiastic crowds and they cheer as though God had given us a blessing.

Love to all, yr. loving son,
Stanley

John Edgar MacElrath lived near McMinn, Tennessee, about fifty miles north of Chattanooga. He was the son of a prosperous merchant with southern ancestors for many generations. His mother's family came from Connecticut and traced its lineage to John Alden. MacElrath was three years younger than Stanley.

MacElrath enlisted as a Second Lieutenant in the 3rd Tennessee Mounted Infantry headed by Lillard. The regiment fought in the First Battle of Bull Run (July, 1861) before moving on to the western fronts in Tennessee and Kentucky. Mac rose to the rank of captain and survived the war to return home to Tennessee. He then attended and graduated from law school. Mac and Stanley never did meet in battle, nor did MacElrath write to Stanley, nor did he leave a written record of the leave-taking, nor did MacElrath ever plant foot on northern soil again.

Family anecdotes indicate that MacElrath was a "colorful guy when he was in his 50's and 60's." He was both able and educated. On graduation, Mac headed west to Oakland, California where he practiced law. His wife's grandmother was descended from a Cherokee Indian chief. She convinced MacElrath to return to Tennessee to assist the Cherokees in pursuing their claims against the government. There, he contracted pneumonia and died.[7]

> Beverly
> April 21, 1861

Dear Stanley,

I thank you for your letter, it went to your Mother's heart, and I should have felt just as you did at your young friend's departure. God knows I never before had the kind of heartache I have had today. . . . I know not but last Sunday Henry wrote his last letter to me from his Washington home. It was a sad one truly but today he may be fighting for his life [in the first Battle of Bull Run], if one can credit telegraphic signs. At any rate they seem to be near a struggle there and it is all the more sad because too many on both sides feel like poor MacElrath. . . .

Write just as often as you can, and pour out everything to your mother—her heart will always be open to all your trials of whatsoever sort they may be. I must have the love of all my children. I am afraid something is the matter with your physique if you have had sick headache three days[8]— do take care of the good body your Heavenly Father gave you—it will be disobedience to his laws if you do not.

> Good night and God bless you.
> From yr. loving Mother

Stanley soon faced a decision as to how to participate in the war. The first step was to overcome his father's opposition.

> Cambridge
> April 26, 1861

Dear Father,

Please send me a certificate that you have no objection to my joining a drill company which is being organized by

---

7. From a telephone interview with grandson Charles Black on July 2, 2004, and Confederate Army records.
8. This was the beginning of a series of severe headaches that Stanley would suffer.

the Faculty among the students. Of course, you can have no objections in these times. It will be wholly distinct from the militia and is under the entire control of the college government. Prof. Eliot is to be the chief officer and some say we are to give up afternoon recitations in order to get more time for drill. Please send the certificate by return of mail, if possible, for I don't know how soon I may need it. We are required to have such a certificate from our parents before they will allow us to join. . . .

I have just read over what I have written and I am afraid you will not understand what the nature of this drill company is to be. The college is going to provide drill masters to those of the students who desire to achieve knowledge of the rudiments of military science and all the fellows will join, or at least the vast majority. We are not liable to be called into service and there can be no possible objection to my joining. These are times when every man, or boy who is to be a man, should know how to use his hands in the cause of law. . . . I hope you will not think it necessary to write to make any inquiries for the delay might occasion me considerable inconvenience. I am impatiently awaiting your answer.

Stanley

Cambridge
April 27, 1861

Dear Father,

I see you misunderstood the nature of the drill club. . . . It has not the slightest connection with the State militia and, therefore, from the mere fact that I belong to it, I am no more liable to be called upon than if I had no connection with it at all. Of course, everyone in the state is liable to be drafted but this drill company adds nothing to the probability I shall be called upon.

If I had time I would like to explain to you that I do not sympathize with the South as you seem to imagine.

The cause and the object of this war are two very different things. Not the abolition of slavery but the maintenance of republicanism is the end to be attained by this conflict and as such it becomes every American to be ready to stand by his country in this time of need.

This drill club however has nothing to do with the matter at all. It is entirely a college matter. Edwin has probably explained why I put my name upon the list. It never occurred to me that you could have the slightest objection. In fact, you would have none did you understand the matter for you said in your letter that you would entirely approve of anything of the sort undertaken for exercise, which is the case here.

Love to all from your affec. son,
Stanley

STANLEY'S JOURNAL

May 1, 1861. Today I drilled for the first time. At 12, I went to the Gymnasium where there were at least 200 fellows. They put several graduates and some students over the motley crowd as drill masters but as a general thing they knew almost nothing about the business. We went through the motions for a while and then Perkins led us out upon the [quad] where we maneuvered with great disorder and no small fun until 1 o'clock when we all marched back to the Gymnasium and Prof. Eliot made us a speech about the Arsenal.

All above 21 can volunteer; all below must bring a written certificate from their parents that they are willing they should serve and I was therefore obliged to write to Father.

May 6, 1861. This noon and evening I drilled. We are actually getting to look quite soldier like. We ran all round the Gymnasium this evening at double quick pace going through the motions at the same time with our muskets. As there were some 200 of us, the regular and rapid beat of steps, the rapid motion, and the sight of the bayonets gleaming brightly in the flashing gaslight quite excited me. What a strange feeling it is to sympathize in motion, sound, or sight with a multitude. Self is lost and yet consciousness is quickened. No wonder dances and rapid motion were parts of the mad revels of the bacchanals—nothing intoxicates more.

———

Cambridge
June 16, 1861

Dear Mother,

It is Sunday morning and it is well named. It is the sun's day with a vengeance. I think old Phoebus has the measles or something of the sort and, being unable to run the coach himself, has committed it to the care of some rash Phaethon who is making strait for the colleges. The feet bake on the pavement and the soles of my shoes are almost singed. I am in a sea of trouble, (which I am about to take sponge against), i.e. perspiration.

You cannot expect me to write a long letter though for a wonder I have some news to tell you! My chum is probably suspended! He, like a great ninny, joined two other fellows, one of whom was his brother, in screwing up the doors of Holden Chapel, Daniel's room, and Tutor Edwin Hale Abbot's; but the divinity who presides over doors, angry at the repeated insults heaped upon her, effected that her insulters should be detected and caught as they were at work on Ed's door! Gracious powers what a scene! I wish it wasn't too hot to invoke some pitying muse to my aid in describing it! They (that is the offenders) rushed into my room waking me up. They were followed by two indignant constables and an immense bulldog. Soon Edwin appeared in his nightgown with a shawl thrown over his shoulders. Meenbus Schmidtts, the German master, stalked down the entry like Hamlet's ghost in a flowing German robe and smoking cap.

The three culprits stood huddled together, the implements of their "guy" in their hands and your humble servant, attired in robes of purest white, completed the picture. What varied expressions appeared on the faces of the different actors of the scene from blowhard, the pussy constable, to meekness, the youngest offenders!

After a most severe examination the miserable wretches were left alone with misery and they have spent the remaining time in useless regrets, I suppose. All this took place last Friday night and they are to learn their fate tomorrow.

Stanley

Hale first became acquainted with John Witt Randall in 1850. Randall and his sister, Belinda, lived near the Abbots in Boston. He frequently visited the Abbot house on Saturday evenings. Randall had no children of his own, and became a close friend of all the Abbot children in a kind of avuncular relationship.

Stanley and Frank on separate occasions enjoyed a hike with Randall through the White Mountains. Each visited Randall's house frequently while in college. On Randall's death, he bequeathed the income from a trust fund to Frank to use in part to publish a book with Randall's poems, *Poems of Nature and Life*. The Introduction to the book includes letters between Randall and Stanley's brother, Frank.[9] Randall also bequeathed to Hale such of his collection of prints and etchings as Harvard did not want. After spending four generations gathering dust in family attics the prints and etchings were sold to help finance this book. I think both Randall and Stanley would be pleased.

STANLEY'S JOURNAL

June 28, 1861. I went to Mr. Randall's toward evening. He and I walked down to the Station from which the 10th Regt. was going to start for the war. When we arrived they

---

9. John Witt Randall, *Poems of Nature and Life* (Boston: George H. Ellis, 1899).

had already got into the cars, and at least twenty-one or two were filled with them.

The streets and Station were crowded with women, many of them weeping bitterly, and when the train slowly started passing along between two dense crowds of poor sobbing wretches, who stood on both sides of the cars, waving their miserable dirty handkerchiefs, or bonnets, or whatever they had, and when the poor fellows in the cars leaned half way out the windows cheering and shouting out "Goodbye to ye, honey" whenever anyone happened to see his sobbing sweetheart, I could not help feeling a thrill of indignation at the scoundrels who have headed and precipitated the secession movement. Ah! They will have a heavy debt to pay! . . . I staid all night, and Mr. Randall walked out with me in the morning from Boston.

CHAPTER 7

—∞∞—

BRAIN FEVER
JULY, 1861–NOVEMBER, 1861

Men hang out their signs indicative of their respective trades . . .
but up in the mountains of New Hampshire, God Almighty has
hung out a sign to show that there He makes men.
—DANIEL WEBSTER
On the Old Man of the Mountains

Stanley completed his freshman year uncertain of the future.
The first step was a hiking trip through the White Mountains
with John Witt Randall. The arrival of college grades revealed
that Stanley did not qualify for scholarship aid. Furthermore,
Henry and Edwin said they could not afford to continue paying
Stanley's college expenses without the scholarship help. Stanley's journal on August 16 expressed a determination to "go
South," i.e., join the Union Army. Nevertheless, he returned
to his room at Harvard to start his sophomore year. There is
no record of how he could afford to do this. Edwin probably
agreed to provide the financing and certainly influenced the
decision.[1]

Shortly after classes began, Stanley's headaches worsened.
He was "threatened with brain fever" that the doctors could

---

1. See Stanley's journal dated August 31, 1861 on page 83.

not cure other than with lots of rest.[2] Stanley returned to the family in Beverly where Father Hale had accepted in April the position of first principal of the Beverly High School.

Stanley's ongoing conflict with his father influenced Stanley's decision, after two months at home, to continue his recuperation at the Abbot Homestead in Wilton, New Hampshire. Edwin later quoted Mother Fanny as advising Stanley not to return home "both because Father finds money so hard to get that he cannot afford it and because you are not careful enough to treat him with due respect and to control yourself in his company."[3] Stanley looked on the Wilton interlude as a necessary step to recover strength so as to pursue his desire to become an officer in the Regular Army.

STANLEY'S JOURNAL

July 12, 1861. I am no longer a freshman! Well I am not very proud of my sophomore honors. I think I shall continue to walk the earth and the stars will be in no danger of being knocked down by my aspiring headache. . . . Examinations are through and I have time to feel how tired I am. This afternoon, I went to see Rice and stayed there until I was late at supper. We talked of books and college and the best sort of government, he declaring that Republicanism was the most desirable and I that that was to be preferred which most perfectly secured the safety of life and property at the cheapest rate. And so has passed the first day of my sophomore year. I am sleepy, and tired, and blue, and unwilling to think about the future.

2. "Brain fever describes a medical condition where a part of the brain becomes inflamed and causes symptoms that present as fever. The terminology is dated, and is encountered most often in Victorian literature. Conditions that may be described as brain fever include: encephalitis . . . [and] meningitis." http://en.wikipedia.org/wiki/brain_fever. Last updated October 15, 2011.

3. See letter to Stanley from Edwin dated February 24, 1862 on page 112.

July 23, 1861. Summit of Mt. Washington. Yesterday
Mr. Randall and myself came up from Portland to Gorham,
and spent the night at the stage house. My head ached
terribly in the cars. At So. Paris the mountain scenery
begins. Before reaching that place, the country is the
dreariest and most uninteresting I ever saw. It is not until
you get to Gilead or Bethel that the stately Mr. Moriah
frowns upon you and the lovely valley of the Androscoggin,
with the delightful river, fascinates you on the right.

From Bethel, as you pass through Gilead and Shelburne,
the scene momently grows more lovely until, at Gorham,
Mt. Madison rises magnificently on your left and, at points,
the double peaks of Mt. Washington appear. . . . Much to
my joy, [it] was decided upon to climb Mt. Washington and
we started at about 9 upon our walk. The Glen road is very
beautiful and we had very fine views of Mt. Madison and
Washington on the right and Mt. Moriah and the Carter
mts. on our left at different points upon the route. . . .

And now, the road ends and we pass on vigorously for
the top—Top House is in sight! We scramble over the rocks
like squirrels and at last, oh joy! We stand on the topmost
stone to see—nothing! A vast bank of cloud reached the
mountain top at the same moment with ourselves and in five
minutes we were in a room of cloud, fairly in the Heavens!
We could not see fifty yards in any direction not even down
the mountain! A pretty reward for all our toil! . . .

The clouds are mostly dissipated. We may see
something yet! They are dispersed toward the setting
sun, whose horizontal beams light the dark tops of Mts.
Adams, Madison and Jefferson that stand a stately trio like
Titans holding solemn council with themselves! A thousand
peaks, as far as eye can reach, are rendered lurid by the
illuminated mist of the evening and the gorgeous sky bends
to an earth hardly less brilliant than itself. It is an ocean of
green and blue and purple. Two hundred miles I can see in
all directions, 160,000 square miles! The sun is sinking in
blood red clouds. I can write no more. I must be all eye!

I am stupid with fever and headache.

North Conway
August 8, 1861

Dear Stanley,

I am sorry to say that you have no chance for a scholarship. You fell ten places in the Class last Term, and are now so low that you have no chance for a scholarship, this year at least, and only very great improvement in fidelity to your duty will enable you to get one next year.

You know how our arrangement was made, and that I borrowed money in my own name to pay your bills during this last year, that I depended on your success and doing what I thought you had both intellectual ability and moral strength enough to do. It appears that our estimate was too high, and I am sincerely sorry that we made the mistake.

I do not propose to say anything of the causes of failure. It is for you to be faithful to yourself and see where the trouble lies. It is necessarily either a weak head or a weak heart and I hope that God will guide you to see the truth, and really to know yourself, and learn by this bitter result where the weakness is and how to remedy it.

I write now to say that I have every wish to help you, as you know, but I am unable to continue our last year's arrangement, trusting to a scholarship for next year's work. The element of doubt is too great. It is not nearly so easy to succeed next year as it was last, and I have little hope that you will succeed then when you have failed now. . . .

I am simply sorry, grieved, that you have failed where you desired and might have obtained success. I feel that the responsibility rests with you for the past and the future. I earnestly wished to help you and perhaps was too ready to assume the work of providing money for the past year in order to smooth your path and ensure what I deemed almost certain success by relieving you from pecuniary care and anxiety and leaving your mind wholly free for your college duties. . . .

The points which I would propose for your consideration are these. Do not let mere inclination rule, but be wise, for your decision involves so much.

1st—Are you not wrong in imagining yourself fit for an education? It is no luxury in which you can indulge unless duty is clear. You say you have done your best. You said so at the Dixwell's school. Your success there and here was about the same. All the discipline of the past four years has not improved your scholarship. Are you on the right track?

2nd—What do you propose for the future? 1st as to kind of work? 2nd as to support in doing it?

I hope you will seriously and earnestly reflect on these questions. You are nearly a man. You must show yourself one. Your future is in your own hands.

Your brother,
Edwin

STANLEY'S JOURNAL

August 16, 1861. I have not written here for a long, long time—but perhaps it is better the whole story of these 16 days should be told connectedly. . . .

I found my laziness had lost me the scholarship, which I might have got with all ease if I had studied. I am determined to go South. . . .

I do not think I shall live many years, perhaps not months, for I have made up my mind to throw myself body and soul into this war. I will shun no danger, fear no risk. I am indifferent whether I live or die. I know right well, if I do live, I shall accomplish what I aim at, a great name and great usefulness as a writer, but I shrink sometimes at the dreary waste my personal history bids fair to be and would fain sleep for ages. I am not vain. I know what I can do and "know myself" though that does not make me very wise.

August 31, 1861. I went home, had a talk with Edwin, and returned with him to Cambridge in the afternoon, almost decided to go back to college, for he was very kind to me. I did not however promise him or bind myself in any way. I am free. I got my room to rights on Thursday. On

Friday went in to Sophocles. For the first time recited as a Soph.

—————

> Cambridge
> Wednesday morning
> September [n.d.], 1861

Dear Edwin,

I have been a little unwell. Monday as I came out of 3rd recitation my head felt very queerly. . . . I started into town and did not recover myself until I got to the bridge. I came home at once. Next day I had a very bad headache and after breakfast I fainted today. I have just had a little return of the weirdness. My head aches still very much and I don't exactly understand what is the matter with me. I am not feverish. Will you come to see me? Nobody knows about my head, so don't say anything to anyone.

> Yours,
> Stanley

—————

> Beverly
> September 26, 1861

Dear [Sister] Em,

You must think me a miserable scoundrel not to have written to you after my promise but "circumstances" did really prevent this time. Fact is I have got some tiresome bother about my head. It aches obstinately and all that sort of bore; Ed got frightened and brought me down to Beverly *vi et armis,* that is to say by persuasion and the cars. Dr. Torrey has now captured me and if I don't escape some one of these cool nights I don't know when I shall get out of his clutches.

It isn't a place to be jolly in, as perhaps you may be aware, this Beverly of ours! And I am not jolly but it might be worse. I do really hope I shall get back to Cambridge in a week or two but I am getting discouraged. [My] headache is getting worse if anything and I could not have a worse job to do than the making up of my sophomore first term studies. It is absolutely impossible to maintain one's standing in making up to say nothing of gaining.

The worst of the business is that I feel well enough except this affection of the head. What it is, I don't know nor [does Dr.] Augustus M. T[orrey] either.

Rather complaining and grouchy am I not? Can't help myself. You knew what you bargained for when you asked me to write you. I hate the whole idea of corresponding when there is nothing to say and feel it my duty therefore to make my part of correspondence hateful!

Yr. loving brother,
Stanley

Beverly
November 6, 1861

Edward Stanley Abbot has been under my care during his absence from Cambridge and during that time has been too ill to attend to college duties.

Dr. Augustus Torrey

STANLEY'S JOURNAL

November 6, 1861. How strange to open this book and once more write my record on its pages. Just two months since I wrote the last sentence. I cannot write my record. I can only say I have been sick eight weeks. I have been at home for that time, and while there have read some few books, made a fort and paper soldiers for Willie, and have learned the first volume of Hardee.[4] That is all. How shall I

---

4. Lieut.-Col. W. J. Hardee, *Rifle and Light Military Tactics or the Exercise and Manœuvres of Troops When Acting as Light Infantry or Riflemen* (Philadelphia: Lippincott, Grambo & Co., 1855). This became the best-known drill manual of the Civil War.

explain the change in my thoughts and purposes that have made me a different being?

Sick of a headache for three days after I wrote here last. Dr. Wyman sent me to Beverly to Dr. Torrey. For a fortnight, I staid in bed doing nothing "threatened with a brain fever." For another fortnight, I sat up in an easy chair, my head thinking and aching. For four weeks I was convalescent, reading a few novels, a few magazines, and the newspapers, walking with Joe Torrey and playing euchre[5] with him etc. . . . and getting out of my teens.[6]

I am waiting to see Edwin. I came up in the ½ past 4 train, stopped in the Port at Mrs. Wilson's for supper, came to my room and found my chum, copied some writing and wrote this. Going to bed. Tomorrow will be memorable with me. I shall see Edwin and my fate will be decided.

Edwin, in his legal and controlling manner, signed a formal Agreement with Stanley to be sure that Stanley carried out his wishes.

AGREEMENT BETWEEN EDWIN AND STANLEY

Stanley agrees to go and work on a farm, as Edwin arranges for him, until the first of March, 1862; to give up all head work as far as possible, and not to read or look into a book more than one hour a day by the clock; to avoid discussing his military projects; and to keep this agreement wholly and entirely secret, as well as his plans for the future.

Without reserve and upon honor,
Edward Stanley Abbot

---

5. "Euchre is a trick-taking card game most commonly played with four people in two partnerships with a deck of 24 standard playing cards. It is the game responsible for introducing the joker into modern packs; this was invented around 1860 . . ." http://en.wikipedia.org/wiki/Euchre. Last updated June 7, 2012.

6. Stanley turned twenty years of age on October 22, 1861.

Edwin agrees, in consideration of the faithful and exact fulfillment of the above on Stanley's part, to, after the first of March, if Stanley still wishes coolly and decides deliberately to carry out his military designs, assist him to the best of his [Edwin's] ability, in getting a military education to fit him for an officer's commission, and then, when Stanley is fit for such a commission, to aid him so far as he can, in obtaining one.

> Without reserve and
> upon honor,
> Edwin Hale Abbot

> Done at Cambridge, A.D.
> 1861, November 8

It is also mutually agreed that as long as Edwin tries to get Stanley a commission (supposing him still to desire it), that Stanley will not enlist as a private soldier without Edwin's written approval of his so doing.

Meanwhile, Sister Em reported on Halloween antics among the Pennsylvania Dutch in Meadville, Pennsylvania where she was visiting Brother Frank.

> Meadville, Pennsylvania
> November 6, 1861

My dear brother,

I am afraid you would find it dull—it is a more quiet place even than Beverly—No cars within sixteen miles and one mail a day and, sometime in winter when the traveling is very bad, I believe the mail is often minimus for a day or two at a time. However, for all that, it is a pleasant place. The people manage to see a good deal of each other in a quiet way. There is no end to the running in and out. Now last evening, though a dark, stormy night, we had three people "run in. . . ."

Last Friday was "Hallow Eve" as they call it here and it seems it is a Dutch custom to make it a time of general frolic or merry making. The Hindekopers are Dutch and, in fact, a large part of the people here are Dutch or German by descent. We were invited to Miss Lizzie's to tea on "Hallow Eve" and afterwards to a "taffy making." Miss Lizzie told us she had had all her pumpkins, squashes and other vegetables brought under cover that day or she should have expected to have heard them come against the front door at intervals during the evening, or else put on the spikes of the fence.

I suppose you are just as ignorant what a taffy making is as I was. . . . We all went in calico dresses, and adjourned to the kitchen, where a large pot of molasses was boiling away and we amused ourselves with eating nuts, stirring the candy, and so forth until time to pull it. Now and then we were interrupted by a great turnip coming in at the window or a large stone.

When we went upstairs into the parlor, there was a large pumpkin on the end of a stick to greet us as we entered, placed there by someone, while we were all downstairs. I was more of a spectator than actor in the scene in the kitchen. I was perfectly amazed and infinitely amused at the reckless way in which the sticky stuff was thrown about. Altogether, it was a very funny evening.

Your own sister,
Emmy

STANLEY'S JOURNAL

November 7, 1861. I am going to spend the winter at Wilton or Dunbarton,[7] and in March enter some military school, and by May Edwin thinks he can get me a commission.

This really decides my fate, probably for this world.

---

7. Harris Ryder, a cousin of Stanley's mother, lived in Dunbarton, New Hampshire and is not to be confused with Harris Abbot, a brother of Stanley's father, who lived on the Abbot Homestead in Wilton, New Hampshire.

Stanley had a remarkable ability to dislike an individual's positions or actions while still admiring his integrity. In the journal entry below, he admired both the southerners and abolitionists while disagreeing with their positions. He made the same sort of statement about southerners when discussing the parting with MacElrath.[8] Stanley would have agreed with Lincoln's statement in his Second Inaugural Address: "with malice towards none, and charity for all." Part of Stanley's upbringing and self-image was to consider himself a gentleman. This desire also appeared in the following journal entry.[9]

STANLEY'S JOURNAL

November 14, 1861. The war is a question of policy and I cannot sufficiently admire the self-devotion and energy displayed by the South at this time of their dire distress. I have not words to express my contempt for those braggarts among us who think that patriotism means the systematic blackguarding of the really chivalrous gentlemen of the South who support their cause so gallantly.

I think they are mistaken, but I feel no desire to deny them the hearty respect I accord to Wendell Phillips and consistent abolitionists. I believe them to be all mistaken but their honest mistakes and the hearty support they afford their bad causes should teach us to be still more heroic and unselfish in our fidelity to our good cause.

If I go south it will be without any animosity against those I am to fight. On the contrary I will try to admire and love them for their generous manliness but not therefore will I fight the less stubbornly and bravely. I shall remember that, while I struggle with noble gentlemen, I also am a gentleman and with the better cause. Victory over these antagonists will be glorious indeed!

---

8. See letter to Mother from Stanley dated April 19, 1861 on page 71.
9. See letter to Edwin from Stanley dated March 12, 1862 on page 121. "Don't fear I will forget I am a gentleman because I may have a ditch to dig."

November 15, 1861. Today I have been packing up all my things; some of which I am to send to Beverly, others I am [sending] to Wilton. Oh dear, what a fool I am. I do get so attached to place! College looks so beautiful to me now.

I am to leave it forever. It is a real sacrifice I am making, I think, for I dread the life before me every way very much. All my tastes are with books and it seems terrible to me to postpone my prospect of writing. I know that I can write well in time, though no one can be better aware than I am that everything thus far has been "veal."[10] I know that I have talent and I long to exercise it. Yet I dare not publish in my own name things I would blush to own hereafter. I will never acknowledge what I have written thus far. I am safe, for not even in this book have I mentioned about my writing.

Why I have done so is more than I can say—but I have a strange feeling that this may yet be read by someone. Edwin perhaps.—Well, neither my silliness, nor ____'s fault is betrayed here, and should he read it he will not know ____'s name. What a brute the fellow is to be sure! He is not worth a tithe of what I did for him. Well, thank my good fortune, I never counted on much gratitude—but really it is a bit disappointing![11]

---

10. Stanley uses "veal" several times in the sense of immature, like a calf. Modern dictionaries do not show this meaning. However, according to Rob Kyff, "The Word Guy": "I did find one dictionary entry for 'vealy,' an adjective dating to 1767 meaning 'immature.' It is a logical extension to say that someone was 'vealy' or 'veal.'"
11. See discussion of the incident on page 65.

CHAPTER 8

THE WINTER OF MY DISCONTENT
NOVEMBER, 1861–FEBRUARY, 1862

Now is the winter of our discontent.
—WILLIAM SHAKESPEARE, *King Richard III*

The historical and emotional center of Stanley's extended family was the Abbot Homestead on Abbot Hill in Wilton, New Hampshire. Fanny, an only child, was welcomed into Hale's large family and she maintained an extensive correspondence with Hale's siblings and parents. Stanley was well-acquainted with his uncles, aunts, and cousins from summer visits to the homestead as a child. Stanley's letters to cousin Emily Knight comprise a large part of Chapter 3. Following the death of her father in the early 1850's, Emily and her mother resided at the Homestead with Rebekah Hale Abbot (Stanley and Emily's grandmother) and Harris Abbot (Stanley and Emily's uncle).

Since Stanley did not want to remain in Beverly and face the ongoing conflicts with his father, it was natural for him to seek refuge at the Abbot Homestead where he would be welcomed and accepted by his extended family.

Uncle Harris, the most enterprising of Hale's siblings, inherited three-fourths of the Abbot Homestead on his father's death with the charge "to see to it that his brothers and sisters never came to distress."[1] Uncle Nelson inherited the other

---

1. Charles G. Abbot, *Uncles* (Washington: Self-published, 1949), 2.

ABBOT HOMESTEAD
Wilton, New Hampshire

quarter.[2] Charles Greeley Abbot, a son of Harris and Annie, recalled, "In my time, we had a free hotel in summer. We used to sit down at table with over 20 persons, many of them visiting relatives."[3]

Uncle Harris was forty-eight when he married Auntie Annie, who was twenty-four, in 1860. They had no children of their own when Stanley, now twenty, came to live with them a year later. Uncle Abiel was unmarried and also lived at the

---

2. Abbot Hill followed the ultimogeniture inheritance practice of southeast England where the family emigrated from in the 1640's. It made it more likely that the younger sons would inherit so that the older sons could become better educated, move the family ahead, marry, and move out. Thus the eldest son did not have to wait for the old folks to let go of the reins. Hale, the oldest son, attended college, while his younger siblings, Harris and Nelson, inherited the family farm. Elinor Abbot, e-mail message to the author, July 2, 2010.

3. Abbot, *Uncles*, 2.

family homestead. Harris and Annie's son, Charles Greeley Abbot, recollected that "Years went on, while Uncle 'Bial dozed by the fireplace, or wrote in his diary, or read the thermometer, or carried on his other urgent occupations."[4]

A fellow townsman, referring to the intellectual standing of the family, stated that, "The Abbots have an *infinite* capacity for the consideration of a subject." Stanley's mother, Fanny, perhaps with Uncle 'Bial in mind, revised the saying to, "The Abbots have an infinite capacity for the *consideration* of a subject."[5]

Other aunts, uncles, and cousins, who appear frequently in Stanley's writing, lived nearby on Abbot Hill.

Stanley's next journal entry appeared after his arrival at the Abbot Homestead.

STANLEY'S JOURNAL

November 21, 1861. We had a beautiful sunset, and I enjoyed it amazingly standing upon the barn yard fence, until my raptures were interrupted by a miserable little cockerel, who strutted about as if he were lord of creation, making a terrific racket. I thought I would humble him so I imitated his crow, I flatter myself, with some skill. This irritated his majesty sorely and he crowed defiantly again and again. Each time he was answered by a louder peal from his new and unlooked for rival. At last I triumphed, and he ingloriously fled to his seraglio with his throat even sorer than mine, I hope and suspect.

Tonight Uncle Abiel is going to improvise a set of chess men, with which I hope to play.

November 23, 1861. Yesterday I stayed in much of the day, making knights for Uncle Abiel's chess men, which I flatter myself I did in rather an artistic manner. Uncle takes much interest in the progress of the work.

---

4. Ibid., 4.
5. Ibid., 3.

In the evening he and I started off to go to Squire
Abbot's where we had admired Venus long enough to
almost get to the school house. We saw that ugly edifice
brilliantly illuminated. We went as far as the door, and
looking in, I saw Louisa sitting on one of the benches
looking just as when I took leave of her four long years
ago. How strange it seems to come to Wilton, and
seemingly take up the life and thoughts of years gone by!
What a change these eight and forty mos. have made in
me. I seem a different being internally and externally—the
seeds I had but just planted then have ripened and borne
fruit of bitterness and sorrow. I know that I am a man—and
I remember the boy I was of old.

How old thoughts and feelings rushed back on me
as I stood in the darkness looking on the fair face that
seemed to gaze on me as a phantom from the past, and
thoughts of the possible future flashed across my mind, and
I shuddered as I walked away haunted by the spirit ghosts
of what has been and what may be. Time keeps his secrets
well, but he shall declare them yet.

November 24, 1861. After supper Uncle Harris, Jack,
Uncle Abiel and myself had a curious discussion about how
much corn could be got into the sitting room where we
were. After much calculation we determined it would hold
about 1446 bushels. We had quite a nice time and a good
deal of laughter over it.

Wilton
November 24, 1861

Dear Mother,

I write this on top of the iron fireplace in the sitting
room, shivering with cold. I have just got back from church
to a house innocent of fires and by consequence of heat
and by consequence of comfort in this winter weather with
the ground covered with newly fallen snow.

What a horrible hole a country church is, to be sure!
Atrociously hot and uncomfortable also by reason of those
ingenious implements of torture—strait backed pews
reaching nearer heaven than the most pious aspirations

of the agonized saints that are being martyred by them.
Add to this a stupid preacher and a cattish choir and if you
don't pity me your heart is harder than I take it to be—for
I have endured all these inflictions for three weary hours
this day.

Well, here I am in Wilton, once more booked for a
three month's stay here, I am afraid. I use the last word not
because I apprehend having a bad time but because I hate
to put off the carrying out of my plans for so long a time.
However, since I am to be banished, I prefer this place to
any other. . . .

Now about Aunt Annie—well she is tall and quite good
looking, auburn hair, light blue eyes, fair complexion and
a neat dress—voila the mistress of the old homestead. She
is really very pleasant and kind, inclined to be silent when
others will talk but perfectly capable of talking well and
intelligently if she pleases. . . . Actually, she has literary
tastes. How came she to marry Uncle Harris? 'Tis the
[unlikeliest] of all I have ever seen that bids fair to be the
happiest. . . .

I am well and my head has ached less since I have
been here than I could have expected. Though, of course,
it still troubles me somewhat; likewise the remains of
a cold.

Love to Grandfather and the rest.
Your affec. son, Stanley

STANLEY'S JOURNAL

November 30, 1861. On Thanksgiving Day I went
to church and headache itself was unable to spoil my
enjoyment of the Baptist parson's sermon. It is impossible
to give an idea of the man's absurdity. He talked of the
country being "rampant and unruly"—Said that a certain
amount of prayer must be offered up if we were to succeed
in the war and, as the men in power would not pray, he
exhorted his hearers to take a double job in hand to make

up the deficit and finally he prayed we might "be too many guns for the South" in those exact words. But why should I attempt to give an idea of what is indescribable? . . .

After dinner we played proverbs etc. and in the evening all the singers gathered round the melodeon and sang. How strange it is. Cheerful music always makes me sad and, while they were singing, I had a terrible fit of the blues! I thought of my own future until I worked myself up into perfect foam. I curled myself into a corner by the fireplace, and was miserable until Aunt Annie came to me and said "A penny for your thoughts" in so kind and sympathizing a way that I loved her for it and roused myself partially—and yet my unaccountable depression would not be driven away wholly. Who can explain these phenomena of feeling? Surely not I. . . .

This morning I took a walk on the Milford road and thence across the hill and woods to the house with Uncle Abiel. It snowed last night, and today the branches of all the trees are loaded with whiteness and beauty. I declare the winter is as beautiful as summer in the country and the snow is a marvelous good adorner.

———

Wilton
November 30, 1861

Dear Mother,

I hasten to write you before "the winter of my discontent" fairly sets in. I don't like the prospect of being buried in the snows of a New Hampshire winter without a requisite motive but one must pay in this world for carrying out darling projects and I don't know as a 3 month's annihilation is a dear price to pay for the accomplishments of mine. But the less I think and write about that the better I suppose.

My head has bothered me considerably lately but I hope to get rid of my headaches in time. *Basta.*

Yr. loving son Stanley

———

Wilton
December 3, 1861

Dear Edwin,

There is, of course, nothing to say about Wilton or
Wilton folk. The place is covered with snow. The people
are well. I am quite getting into favor with Aunt Annie who
I like ever so much. She is very kind and obliging and,
though silent, still very pleasant company in the evening
where we are all gathered round the fire talking about the
little nothings that seem to interest them all here. I can't
say that I have as yet any great interest in the affairs of
Mr. Eliphalet Putnam[6] nor yet in the progress of the new
Mason[7] road about which the Wilton world is all agog,
but still I am not so much like a fish out of water as I
suspected I would be.

Your loving brother,
Stanley

Stanley had been at the Abbot Homestead for about a
month with his activities limited by the agreement with Edwin
as well as by his headaches. This left lots of time to reflect on
his past, current, and future life, including the impact on his
life of the conditions in his country.

It was a "very windy and cold" Sunday morning with all
sitting around the living room fire. Stanley used the time to
break the family rule of secrecy and write Sister Em to "give
you some idea of myself." This important letter is quoted in
full below in its chronological setting while pieces of it are
repeated elsewhere throughout the book, as appropriate.

Wilton
December 15, 1861[8]

Dear [Sister] Em,

It is very windy and cold so no one has thought of
going to church and we are all gathered round the sitting

---

6. A cousin.
7. Mason, New Hampshire is the town just south of Wilton.
8. Portions of this letter are repeated on pages 2 and 214.

EMILY FRANCES ABBOT
1839–1899

room fire. The question naturally arises "what shall we do with ourselves"? Each solves it in his own way, Uncle Harris is asleep in his chair, Uncle Abiel is reading the "Tribune," Aunt Annie is combing her hair and I—I am writing to Em.

I want to give you some idea of myself, for I may never have so good an opportunity. Secretiveness is the rule of our family. I wish to prove that rule by making an exception to it, a la old saw.

I will begin with outside matters. Please keep them secret. In the first place, I have taken up my connections at college not because I have abandoned my design of becoming a writer should I live. That I still cling to unalterably, as I have ever since I first entertained the idea of going to Cambridge. But, because I am going to enter the army, I shall stay at Wilton until March, a long time but still necessary for I mean to give myself a fair chance to get through the war alive and I am now neither strong nor well. I must be both before it would be right for me to expose myself to the hardships of a campaign.

I am not one of those lack-a-daisical would-be-heroes who consider that a soldier's duties can be fulfilled by simple, romantic bravery. I know perfectly well that courage is only a small part of what is needful. Strength, health, knowledge of the business are indispensable—I shall acquire them.

After I have recovered myself fully, which I shall have done by March, I trust and believe, I shall enter a military school, where I shall be from two to three months. At the expiration of that time Edwin has promised to do his best to get me a commission and I do not doubt he will succeed. He is himself confident that he will.

Should he fail, which I most earnestly hope he will not do, I shall enlist as a private. My reasons for this you, of course, know. I suppose you must have thought me very easily influenced when I apparently went back to college but from the first I have made up my mind that I must go. I wished to prove that I was not going because I was dazzled by brass buttons, as you all thought. That is the sole reason of my delay for, in truth, the respect of my friends is dear to me.

I will not pretend that Edwin approves of the plan. He does not, but if I go at all he thinks this the best way. He earnestly desires me to give up the whole plan but we must each walk by the light that is given us and I cannot give it up unless I also give up my honor. I frankly tell you what I have not told him [Edwin]. I do most heartily wish I could stay at home. It cost me a great deal of suffering to give up my college course but I consider the question as simply a test to my courage and manliness.

The question we have to decide is simply this: shall America in the coming centuries when her children are numbered by hundreds of millions be desolated by long and bloody wars such as have been the agony and have assured the slavery of Europe since her history began? I for one say "No." It can be avoided by maintaining one great empire through the length and breadth of the continent. To maintain this empire is worth their every sacrifice it is within the power of the people to make. No price that can be paid is too high, and now the question comes up, can we maintain the cause for which we are fighting? Have we the physical power to do that? I own I am in painful doubt.

I fear the chances are against us. At any rate, if we do succeed, it will be after a struggle more bitter and desperate than any recorded in history. It will be by the exercise of every power we are master of. Every man that can strike a blow will be bitterly missed if he dare not come forward in his country's time of agony—I cannot be such a man, Em. I think it is a glorious thing when one has a chance to be a hero.

I used to read, when I was a little boy, of brave and noble men and wish that I might be a brave and noble man myself. . . . The possibility of becoming such is offered once to each and all. Woe to him that dare not grasp at the prize when it is within his reach.

I love to write. I think whatever abilities I have are such as would fit me to become an author. Sometimes I have fancies that seem to me very beautiful and I think that if I live and grow better I can sometime write such good things that those who read them will become a little better men and women, but I am as certain as I am of my existence that if I become bad and a coward that my beautiful fancies will leave me and that what I write will be utterly wrong, that the mission I believe in my heart that I have will be unfulfilled, and that my life will be a miserable failure.

Now you know what I mean when I say that I dare not stay with my hands folded while this struggle is going on. He that would save his life shall lose it. My life is dear to me; and I know that you and Frank will say "God bless you, you are right" when you read this. I do want sympathy ever so much. I have not had much so far.

They don't trust me much at home. They think I want to be a "gay soldier boy." It is really hard and bitter to know that Mother thinks I am so boyish. Henry, of course, doesn't know much of me and Edwin is a creedist and thinks they are going wrong whose faces are not turned to the New Church, but Mother ought to know me better than they.[9] Don't you and Frank join the rest.

Yr. loving brother Stanley

STANLEY'S JOURNAL

January 1, 1862. A New Year and where will it find me when it too is dying? I wish it may be far South by that time. More extravagant wishes than that have been gratified ere this. Who can say this will not be?

I sat by the fire that died with the waning year and when the white ashes covered the glowing embers like death shrouds, the old house clock in the corner tolled the requiem of dead sixty-one.

---

9. The New Church was based on the theological writings of Emanuel Swedenborg. http://en.wikipedia.org/wiki/New_Church. Last updated September 11, 2011.

What a year this has been. Memorable in history it will be, and in my life—it is the end of my boyhood—henceforth, the work and troubles of manhood will be mine. Ah! How I look back and stretch my hands toward the child life that is no more!

Wilton
January 1, 1862

Dear Edwin,

My head does not trouble me now at all. For about two weeks I have not the vestige of a headache. . . . Do not for a moment think the winter passed here will alter one jot of my determination. I am more and more firmly rooted in the conviction that it is right and inevitable that I should go. My head is well and the object of my stay here is accomplished. Why then should I drone on? I have got strength too. Let me use it. I would not write this if I were not sure that nothing, absolutely nothing can be gained by my part to stay here. Do listen to reason.

Do you still think you have any reasonable chance of being able to get me a commission? Things are getting settled now and most if not all the officers will be taken from the ranks. *N'est ce pas?*

Yr. loving brother Stanley

Wilton
January 5, 1862

Dear Mother,

Every morning I carry Uncle Nelson's children to school and take his horse Charlie who is the most tough-mouthed beast I ever drove.[10] It requires nearly my whole

10. Uncle Nelson resided in a separate house on the Abbot Homestead and farmed a portion of it. He had three children age twelve and under in January, 1862.

weight on one rein if I want to turn him. He goes like the wind, however, and I enjoy my daily rides much.

Ever yr. loving son,
Stanley

———✎———

Wilton
January 5, 1862

Dear [Sister] Em,

You think there is no need of more men. You probably are not aware of the immense proportion of soldiers disabled or killed in the course of even an uneventful campaign, which deficit has to be made good by constant recruiting. . . . It will be a most difficult thing to keep the army as large as it now is and it ought to be vastly increased and will have to be, for a surety, before the Rebellion is finally crushed. So you see "the men are needed."

Besides, we are all vain. The difference between men is simply one of degree of vanity and my vanity is large enough to make me feel confident that I could make a good officer and I should go with, I hope, higher motives than many. If we succeed in putting down the insurrection, the army will have become a tremendous engine of political power and it will be of vital necessity that its weight be thrown on the right side that it should be composed of men who will feel that they are citizens, as well as soldiers, for in their hands will be the destinies of America.

This is no groundless fear, this apprehension of the future course of the army, but a matter for the gravest thought and foreboding. Let us suppose our army triumphant, as perhaps they may be, we shall then have done no more than many a people has accomplished before. But after that public security has been restored by the sword, we shall have a problem to solve to which heretofore there has been but one solution. "How shall public security be maintained"? The unvarying reply has ever been "by the sword." But this answer will never do for us. If that be our fate, submission to military despotism, then is Republicanism an utter failure in our country, and the crushed Rebellion will indeed have wrought our utter destruction.

But it will not do to accept the past as an infallible test of the future. In many important respects we totally differ from all nations which have given their verdict on this question and it is just possible (we can hardly put it stronger) that the consummate glory of self-conquest may await our country after it has gained the dangerous power of a military people.

Now it is evident that all the danger will spring from the army. In the army, then, is the place for the man who loves his country well enough to wish to serve her even at the price of self-immolation. Their influence and talent which would be of no avail elsewhere may be of inestimable value if used to aid on the mighty effort which I have faith to believe will be made to preserve our . . . liberties. The shattering of the insurrection is but a tithe of the work before us. Pray heaven there may be virtue and courage enough in the army to destroy itself when its mission shall have been accomplished!

Talk of "reserving myself." Why, Em, the duty of joining in this struggle seems to me so daylight clear that I can hardly understand your doubts. I feel almost as if I had a mission to accomplish so plainly do I see the path of duty. The object of the war against the South, and our selfishness, seems to me a holy one. One could kneel to pray before battles fought this cause. As for the personal temptations I shall meet in the discharge of this sacred duty, why should I think, or care for them?

The only true way to live is to forget ourselves. Self-denial is not enough. Self must be annihilated, ignored. I would as soon think of shrinking back for fear I might lose a limb or my life as of hesitating lest "my morals" may be impaired. A fig for the virtue that may not be exposed to the dust and heat of the contest, a heavy encumbrance not worth the wearing!

You ask me if I am ambitious a little in this my desire. Yes, I am ambitious. Every thought and feeling is doubly steeped in ambition. Every nerve and drop of blood tingles with it. It is my life, my breath, the condition of my existence. Take from me ambition and I am nothing. I glory in it and am proud of it because I trust and in my very soul believe that it is not a mean and selfish and vulgar ambition. . . .

Since God has given me life and strength to this cause, I must devote my life, consecrate my strength. I must work for it, live for it, die for it. If such happiness should be in store for me, I am happy and proud that I have been thought worthy to live in the hour of the nation's agony. . . . Don't doubt any more, Emmie dear.

Yr. own brother,
Stanley

Wilton
January 10, 1862

Dear Mother,

You ask what are people doing up here? They are one and all simply vegetating, only that and nothing more. They are well physically, mentally generally as far as I can see. Now what more can I say?

Today I went to the examination of the district school. Twenty miserable sprigs of the human family sweated through an investigation into their several proficiency in the three r's ("redin," "ritin" and "rithmetic"). After which that enormous Calvinistic splurge of an orthodox person and 3rd rate dandy, Daniel Adams, having been on compulsion silent for two or three hours, took the opportunity to let off his steam to his great satisfaction and the boring of his unfortunate hearers.[11]

11. Reverend Daniel E. Adams was pastor of the Wilton church from 1860 to 1876. Abiel Abbot Livermore and Sewall Putnam, *History of the Town of Wilton, Hillsborough County, New Hampshire* (Lowell: Marden & Rowell, 1888), 139.

This shaggy haired worthy was followed by my honored uncle, the Rev. Abiel Abbot, who "made a few happy remarks" which closed the Examination.[12] The room was atrociously hot that, though my feet were as cold as ice, the rest of me was par-boiled in sizzling perspiration and by consequence I am enjoying a flourishing young headache at this present moment which fact will, I trust, excuse "any incoherence" etc. etc.

Love to all from
your loving son,
Stanley

———— ✺ ————

Newtonville
January 11, 1862

Dear Stanley,

I am glad you are getting so much better and hope that, by the first of March, you will be really able to enlist or follow any other plan you think wisest and best. But I shall not try to persuade you about it. I am satisfied that now you are too full of faith in your own judgment and knowledge to be led away from your ideas by persuasion or a wish to please those who love you best, and I shall not try it. . . .

You are now nearly a man. As your brother I have tried to save you from error by advice and persuasion. I shall hereafter give you only the former and if you wish not take it, I can only do something useful. But till then keep at it and make a good beginning sure. You must not take it hard that I do not fall in with your enthusiastic projects. They are somewhat like the cry of "On to Richmond." I want you to stick to your bargain and then we will see what can be done. But now, no plans except for dropping wood and gaining strength etc.

---

12. Abiel Abbot was the brother of Stanley's grandfather, Ezra Abbot, and is not to be confused with Uncle 'Bial, who was the brother of Stanley's father, Hale.

Your boyhood is about over. That it has been what I
had expected of you years ago it is useless to pretend. . . .
I acknowledge too that there have been external difficulties
around you and much to call out the evil part of your
nature. . . .

You have now come to the point where you must
look at things true, whether pleasant or not. If you would
yourself, you will then see this truth also: that you really
only pretended to yourself to deny it because either your
own selfish, reckless life must change or such thoughts be
stifled and buried under the ruins of conscience that you
thought you preferred the massacre of the innocents to
the acknowledging of the Messiah, and to still keep your
Herod king rather than to acknowledge the Lord of life.

Your brother,
Edwin

—◦◦◦—

Washington
February 5, 1862

Dear Stanley,

Please send me at once . . . a statement of your desire,
and object for . . . obtaining a commission in the Reg.
U.S. Army,[13] if you have such desire, and wish me to try
to obtain one for you. It should contain a statement of

---

13. Stanley's desire to make a career in the Regular Army was based on
his assumption that, as a Regular Army officer, he would have plenty
of spare time for his true interest, writing. The experience of Lemuel
A. Abbott, author of *Descendants of George Abbott of Rowley, Mass.*,
shows that Stanley may have been wrong on both accounts. Lemuel
was at Norwich University at the same time as Stanley and enlisted
in the 10th Vermont Infantry at the end of July, 1862. At the end of
the Civil War, Lemuel transferred to a Regular Army Infantry unit.
However, he did not write and publish his book until after retirement
from the Army in 1885. William Arba Ellis, comp. and ed., *Norwich
University, 1819–1911: Her History, Her Graduates, Her Roll of Honor*
(Montpelier: Maj. Gen. Grenville M. Dodge, 1911), vol. 2, 682–683.

what you know, what you wish, and why you wish it. A
great deal may depend upon its character and sensible
expression, and it ought to be such as to be proper to
submit to the Secretary of War and to Mr. Wilson, and to
be manly in its tone. Don't write it in red ink.

Send it to me and address it to the Sec. of War, Hon.
Edwin M. Stanton, with all speed and remember that your
best chance of getting a commission through my exertion
will depend very much on your discretion and good sense
now. I think that your chance [of getting a commission] for
months, and probably at all, depends on your conduct at
this juncture. No mere theory of private education for any
purpose will avail here. It will only be given you, if at all,
on the most strenuous exertion and pledge of your desire
to do this work.

> Your brother,
> Edwin

> Washington, DC.
> February 12, 1862

Dear Stanley,

I have just learned from a letter from Mother that you
are gone to Dunbarton. By doing so without notifying
me, as you promised, you have, I fear, lost your best
chance of getting a commission in the Regular Army for
I am forced to leave very soon. I wrote you more than a
week ago to Wilton for a letter from you to the Secretary
of War, applying for a commission and stating what you
know, what you wish, and why you wish it, and have been
watching the mail for it ever since. It was a main object
with me, in deciding me to come here, to forward your plan
and desire and now everything is at a deadlock by your
thoughtlessness in not doing what, in view of just this case,
I asked you to be sure to do and which you promised you
would. I cannot help feeling vexed at your spoiling your
own chances so.

Immediately on receipt of this, please write me such
an application, and with it another full explanatory
letter, suitable to be shown to Mr. Wilson, Mr. Hooper,
Mr. Sumner, Mr. Rice, etc. as indicating your object.[14]
Remember that upon your discretion and good sense now
depend your prospects, for no amount of influence or
management will do anything unless you show yourself
such a man as is wanted for this service. Henry says he
can do nothing and that you must rely on me. If you do
not enable me to work effectively with what you write,
goodbye to any hope of a commission. . . .

I entreat you to act like a man in this business.

Your brother,
Edwin

STANLEY'S JOURNAL

February 13, 1862. I am having a good time here
[Dunbarton]. In the afternoon I usually go to Goffstown
with Harris [Ryder] to get the newspaper, which gives us
something to talk of until after supper, when out comes a
pack of cards and we play euchre, piquet and dominoes
a while. In the morning I read my hour, play with "Cuff"
and the children etc. This has been the usual course of
things. . . .

Edwin wrote me a letter saying I had a chance for a
commission in the Regular Army and asking for a letter
soliciting the appointment and another explanatory one.
I sent both by next mail, and I hope they are such as he
wanted though his own letter was so indefinite I have great
doubts on the subject. I am in a fever of impatience to
learn how he prospers. It would be so completely what I
desire if I could only get it!

---

14. Henry Wilson and Charles Sumner were members of the United
States Senate from Massachusetts. Samuel Hooper and Alexander
Rice were members of the United States House of Representatives
from Massachusetts.

After the war ends, supposing I should survive, I should be stationed in some fort probably, which would give me ample time to prosecute my own plans in writing. I should have a settled support outside of literature, (an inestimable blessing to a litterateur) and should be admirably placed to get a good knowledge of character and affairs, so necessary to a writer in these days. I can only hope I may be successful, and wait-wait-wait; how will it all end?

I long for a new career. A feverish impatience possesses me. My objects remain the same. I shall always pursue them while I live, but the means of attaining these objects I wish to seek in a different way from the one I had marked out for myself. I must be a man, and fight this war through. That is the immediate duty but that accomplished, as a few years at farthest must see it accomplished, and I can honorably take up at once the plans I have temporarily abandoned. It will be too late to return to college and the army is the only place for me if I live, and do not get married. 12 or 15 years from this time (that is, supposing I get my commission) and I may have saved enough to support me. Then I will resign and give my whole time to my beloved plans which, in the meanwhile, I shall not have been obliged to neglect. May I have such a future before me if I live? . . .

Dunbarton, New Hampshire
February 15, 1862

Dear Edwin,

I have just received yours at Dunbarton, New Hampshire the 12th and hasten to reply. I enclose a letter to the Secretary of War applying for a commission in the Regular Army. My reasons for making this application are briefly these. In the first place as you know, I long ago decided that it was my duty to repay that debt of protection which as citizens we all owe to our country in times of peril.

There are usually many ways of serving our country but at the present time for the young and strong there is but one and that is as soldiers in the field. I am young and strong. For me then, the path of duty is clear and unmistakable. Although in the service of our country it is needful to make every necessary sacrifice, yet an unnecessary sacrifice would be a proof of folly rather than of patriotism. Hence, in entering the army, a proper regard to my own interests and to the feelings of my friends requires that I should do so in the manner least prejudicial to my future prospects.

By leaving college at this time I am forced to abandon all my former plans and, at the expiration of the present war, to resume those plans would be impossible without too great a sacrifice of time. No one can afford to learn two trades when he only means to practice one. I have determined then to adopt the military profession and I am most anxious to get a commission in the Regular Army. If I fail in obtaining one in Regular service, I shall try for one in the volunteers and, if still unsuccessful, I shall enlist as a private. For in some capacity I am determined to join in this holier crusade.

As for my ability to perform the duties of a Lieutenant, I have a good knowledge of company movements, having faithfully studied the first volume of Hardee, and then I have had some practical experience of both company and battalion movements in the "Harvard Drill Club" and of the Bayonet exercise in the "Beverly Drill Club." Of course, I shall employ every spare moment in gaining a better knowledge of Tactics etc.

Yr. Affectionate brother,
Edw. Stanley Abbot

Edwin traveled to Washington to further Stanley's wish for a direct commission into the Regular Army. He intended an appeal to President Lincoln as well as to Secretary of War Edwin M. Stanton. A reasonable speculation is that this somewhat personal approach may have been based, in part, on Stanley's or Edwin's acquaintance with Robert Todd Lincoln at Phillips Exeter or Harvard. However, no record exists to support this conjecture.

Washington
February 24, 1862

Dear Stanley,

I leave for Cambridge tomorrow, having stayed to the very last minute in order to push your matter. I received your letter and application which did very well for its purpose. Henry and I have been trying all we can. He has got letters from several officers with whom he has served, and we have gone together to several members of Congress. . . .

The ground on which it has finally become necessary to put it is as a reward for Henry's military service, backed up by political influence.

The Secretary is averse to giving any commission now to persons who have not earned them by service; a mere chance on which it is madness to rely as a reason for entering the ranks. It is therefore exceedingly difficult to get, and you must wait patiently and not fret at delay. We have hurried and pressed the matter as much as possible, but there has been every obstacle in the way.

The death of the President's son has interfered greatly and has cut me off from a personal application to him.[15] Today is the funeral and when Henry went over to the Secretary of War with his papers (for it was best that he as an officer should make the direct application), the office was closed for that reason. I therefore have to leave without knowing how matters stand at the final application.

Even Mother says it will not do for you to come to Beverly any more to stay at present, both because father finds money so hard to get that he cannot afford it and because you are not careful enough to treat him with due respect and to control yourself in his company. He knows nothing of our efforts to get you a commission, and

---

15. William Wallace "Willie" Lincoln, son of President Abraham Lincoln, died from typhoid fever on February 20, 1862 at the age of eleven. http://en.wikipedia.org/wiki/William_Wallace_Lincoln. Last updated August 5, 2011.

HENRY LARCOM ABBOT
1831–1927

I do not wish to broach the subject unnecessarily. And you cannot be at Beverly without telling him about it. Of course; it would make Mother so much trouble not to do so.

As soon as I can learn anything decisive, I will write to you. I have spent much time, trouble, and money in trying to forward this plan of yours and I hope it will succeed since you wish to try a military life. I have no doubt you can make yourself a good and useful officer and we shall do our best to put you on the track. But you must be prepared for failure and non-success.

> With love to all,
> your brother Edwin

CHAPTER 9

EXPECTATION AND DISAPPOINTMENT
MARCH, 1862–JUNE, 1862

Ah, when to the heart of man
Was it ever less than a treason
To go with the drift of things,
To yield with a grace to reason,
And bow and accept the end
Of a love or a season?
—ROBERT FROST, "Reluctance"

March 1st arrived at last, along with good health, freedom from the contract with Edwin that kept Stanley at Wilton, and promised help from Edwin in obtaining a commission. Stanley lost no time in leaving Abbot Hill to pursue a military career in the Regular United States Army.

There is no record of how and why Stanley chose Norwich University in Norwich, Vermont, a small town across the river from Hanover, New Hampshire—the site of Norwich's rival, Dartmouth College. However, the institution, founded in 1819 as the American Literary, Scientific, and Military Academy, is the oldest of the Senior Military Colleges and is recognized by the Department of Defense as the birthplace of the Reserve Officer Training Corps (ROTC). After a catastrophic fire in 1866 which devastated the entire campus, the university moved to the town of Northfield, Vermont, where it stands today.

MRS. DOUE'S HOUSE[1]

Norwich turned out hundreds of officers and soldiers who served with the Union Army in the Civil War. Indeed, the entire class of 1862, including Stanley, enlisted in the Army.[2] In any case, it is clear that Stanley headed there as soon as possible after March 1st.

Wilton
March 1, 1862

Dear Edwin,
The agreement ends today and its object is accomplished. I have not had a headache these five weeks, except one the other day which was entirely the result of the persevering endeavors of little Arthur Abbot[3] to hang on to my hair and ears! . . .

1. Where Stanley stayed while at Norwich, and now known as the Aldrich house.
2. http://en.wikipedia.org/wiki/Norwich_University. Last updated October 28, 2011.
3. This was most likely Arthur Augustus Abbot, son of Isaac Abbot and Harriet Parkhurst. Arthur was a distant cousin born in Wilton on December 6, 1855.

That matter being settled, I want to thank you for your exertions to get me my commission. I don't feel very confident of their success but, whether they succeed or fail, the obligation and my gratitude will be the same. A situation in the Regular Army would be infinitely preferable, of course, to one in the Volunteer. I only hope we may be successful. . . .

The reason why I must leave here is this. I want every moment of time I can get to prepare me for my work. I ought now to be at the military school, studying night and day. . . . Edwin, I cannot speak strongly enough of the imperative necessity there is for carrying out our original plan and agreement. . . . I gave up Harvard in accordance with your advice and I find that I have lost a good deal of my familiarity, even of that little which I learned. Please write the very next mail for I am very anxious to be at my work after this long vegetation . . .

Yr. Loving brother Stanley

⸺◦◦◦⸺

Boston
March 1, 1862

Dear Stanley,

I have not heard from Washington since I left. As yet, I can only repeat what I said that it is best for you to wait a few days at Wilton, until the matter is settled.

Your brother,
Edwin

But again, as mentioned above, Stanley lost no time in traveling to Norwich University after his contract with Edwin expired on March 1st.

Norwich, Vermont
March 6, 1862

Dear Edwin,

Things are getting along "swimmingly" with me. I have passed thro' "school of the soldier" and a dozen other schools so that his highness Gen. Jackman, more familiarly known as "old Jack" or "Jack Trump" (which latter appellation I take to be an abbreviation of "Jack is a trump," as indeed he is), assured me that I "was perfectly competent to command a company of Infantry."

Now I am dipping into Artillery, cramming on the cascabel, the reinforce, the chase and a dozen other parts of the gun.[4] I have gone thru' the drill at the piece and am now practicing the sabre exercise and soon I hope to be able to cut you in pieces after the most approved scientific methods. I am already prepared to lop off your arms by the "Right and Left Morlancets" or to run you thro' in any part of your body you prefer. . . . In fine, I am making glorious progress in the noble art of cutting throats and am already anxious to put my theoretical knowledge to practical application.

Brig. Gen. Jackman of the Vermont Militia is a very good teacher. I suppose, however, he has one serious drawback in teaching Hardee's Tactics. He is himself the author of a Treatise on Infantry Tactics. It is a bad job to set the author of one system to teach another system but then, though, he wastes time by explaining two methods of doing a thing and assuring me that his is by far preferable. Still I get along and that is the main thing.

Yr. brother,
Stanley

Norwich, Vermont
March 8, 1862

Dear Edwin,

Now don't think that I am restless or changeable or anything of the sort—I am simply telling you what Prof. Jackman said to me this afternoon of his own accord,

---

4. The cascabel is a projection behind the breech of a muzzle-loading cannon. The reinforce is the thicker part of a gun barrel, and the chase is the bore of a gun barrel.

without my lisping a word on the subject until introduced by him. Today I finished the study of artillery movements, and, as they are essentially the same as Infantry Tactics in regard to evolutions in section and battery, he only examined me on a few subjects on which he found me informed.

He then said "Mr. Abbot you have now mastered the theory of Infantry and Artillery movements. You have made very rapid progress and have, in a very remarkably short time, learnt what you can learn here with these two exceptions. 1st by remaining here six or eight months, you can pursue a course of Mathematical studies which it would be impossible to pass over in a less time and where I cannot afford the time to carry you thro' as a private pupil which would be both expensive and unnecessary. 2nd by joining the school as a supernumerary you can in the course of 6 weeks or two months have the advantage of perfecting yourself in the manual dexterity in the use of weapons required in your profession but will be no contingency whatever far as actual service is concerned. . . .The tables supply all, and without them Lieut. Maury would be at a loss on the battlefield. . . .

What I want, he says, is to study my tactics until I have them by rote, acquaint myself with the Army regulations, practice the musket and saber exercises I have learnt from him, and if possible accustom myself to drill bodies of men in some drill company. In all of which things he can render me no assistance whatever. . . .

Now what on earth am I to do? I don't know. Where can I take riding lessons? Where can I join a drill company? Now don't let your old doubts of me have sway over you. Believe that this is the advice honestly given me and let me know right off what you think I had best do. He says he can't undertake to carry me thro' the mathematics as a private pupil and he says that if I drill, "I must be in uniform" which would be very expensive.

I am completely at a loss what to do. I shall go on practicing, studying etc. until I hear from you. Where can I go? Or what can I do? Now on one point I want to say a few words. If I should get an appointment in the Artillery, I should be actually unable to get along for the simple reason that I am absolutely and totally ignorant of everything relative to a horse and I should not only be put on one at once but I should be obliged to command a detachment of horsemen!

> Yours in much perplexity,
> Stanley

❊

> Boston
> March 8, 1862

My dear Stanley,

I have just got your letter and am quite puzzled what to answer. The activity of movement at Washington just now has I fear confused our projects and yet any day I may hear from Henry. . . .

If you get the commission, you will have no time to lose, but will undoubtedly join the Regiment at once. It would, if we succeed, be an additional embarrassment & delay to have found any other arrangement. On the other hand, if there is to be no immediate action in the case, the idea of study is a difficult thing. . . .

I fear much on success in the commission and I want you not to set your heart on it. The Chief Clerk in the War Dept. (an old friend of Henry's) told him: "Tell your brother to go back to his studies at College. The Secy. has determined to appoint only from those in active service." This, however, is, if overborne at all, only to be done on strength of Henry's services and of political influence.

> Love to all,
> your Brother Edwin

❊

Boston
March 10, 1862

Dear Henry,

Will you or Susie write me how it is with Stanley's matter now? I enclose his letter to me, just received. I have written to him that I will answer about his coming as soon as I hear from you. I suppose you are very busy now, but Stanley has really a right now to be released from Wilton, unless he is likely to get a commission, and I want to have him settled. His idea is to go to a military school at once and stay till he succeeds in getting a commission. If we agree to this, I think he will be willing to give up enlisting, and wait. And eventually we can get him one, don't you think so?

With much love,
your Brother Edwin

Wilton
March 12, 1862

Dear Edwin,

I have this instant received your letter. Let us consider my position—more than four months ago, I announced to you my final and unalterable determination in respect to this contest. You then made a conditional promise to aid me in my efforts to get a commission and of previously assisting me in my preparation for an officer's career. On the first of March, you bound yourself to aid, according to the best of your ability, me in getting a military education, and verbally this was explained as meaning that I should go to a military school. . . .

At length the time expired and I packed my trunk and hurried to the depot with a joy I never felt before. The clogs were taken off and in a few weeks I hoped to be fitted for my work and on the road to it. . . . I can't "resume my studies." And the reason is not what I fear you esteem it, a boy's impatient whim, but a man's enthusiasm. I am older than you think, not so utterly mean and selfish as one of your recent letters asserted. I really don't much care whether I go with shoulder straps or without them. The main thing is the "go" & the most important thing is "right at once."

Please Edwin let me be four weeks at a school and then let me apply at the state house for a volunteer commission and the moment refusal is given, let me [be] free. Say a "God bless you" and let me be free. Don't fear I will forget I am a gentleman because I may have to dig in a ditch. Don't fear I will disgrace my friends by dishonoring myself. I am conscious that my motives are pure and unselfish & that shall suffice to make me remember not to be a beast. Do not torture me by a longer delay. . . .

Eddie, you really don't do me justice in this matter. I am not dreaming and romancing. This is not theatrical heat, a shabby enthusiasm. . . . I am speaking the truth when I give the lie to that statement of yours that I am not capable of an unselfish act. I know that in this matter self is a secondary consideration entirely. . . . I am honest when I say I am ready to sacrifice my life and my life's ambition to my country if there is need of it.

> With much love,
> Stanley

—∽∾∽—

Boston
March 14, 1862

Dear Stanley,

The difficulty about the school lies here. 1st Three months (as I told you last November) is the shortest time which would avail anything, even for a recommendation to the appointing power. 2nd it is not wise to commit yourself until at least you know the result of our application at Washington. I have watched the mail and expect to hear every day. Until I do hear, I am unwilling to advise anything else. Of course you will do as you please, but it seems to me throwing away about your only chance of really establishing yourself for life.

If the work at Washington has postponed the matter, I should then advise you going to a military school for about three months and waiting for the commission which I strongly believe H[enry] and I can eventually procure you in the Reg. Service. . . .

This project of a commission in the Reg. Army is about your only chance of really establishing yourself for life (which is what I had in mind when I made the agreement, though I did not choose to discuss it at all or suggest it then, for you to dwell upon during your weeks of necessary rest and grow crazy about) is feasible and about the only good one. . . .

As I say this is the plan. At once, if possible, to get a commission in the Army. If delayed, to go for some months to a school where you can learn, and until we can eventually procure a commission. . . .

If you think you can't wait, it is for you to propose something else. I shall consider it very carefully and kindly too. You may be sure anything else is impossible until I know the results of what has cost me absolutely over fifty dollars in cash and nearly three hundred in work which I had to decline.[5] I speak of these things merely to prove to you that I have not been trifling with you as you seem to think. I have, of course, not charged any of this to you. Hereafter, if you are able, you can do what you please, when you have plenty of money.

If you cannot exert more control over your thoughts and keep from fretting, I shall be anxious about your health. You had better go where you will feel easiest except Beverly. I am sorry I cannot do more for you now. You certainly must be greatly excited if you have not a word to say of dear old Grandpa's death.[6]

---

5. Based on cost-of-living data, $350 in 1862 is the equivalent of nearly $8,000 in 2012.

6. Stanley's grandfather Henry Larcom died on February 24, 1862.

I do not see what there is to gain by your coming here, until we know whether the matter has to be postponed at W[ashington]. There is no place for you to come to, no plan to make, and nothing to be done. As soon as I do know, I shall write to you at once.

This project of a commission in the Reg. Army is about your only chance of really establishing yourself for life.

You seem apprehensive that I am not carrying out the agreement. I have merely said that I am and have not gone into detail.

Give my love to all the folks.

Your brother,
Edwin

March 25, 1862

Dear Edwin,

'Tis a vile, ugly village, this Norwich, but the surrounding scenery is (rather in summer will be) very pleasant indeed. . . .

I am writing in the bar room of the "Union Hotel" so you must not expect any very connected epistle. They could not get my room etc. ready before tomorrow so I was obliged to put up for the night at the tavern and a precious poor one it is. However, I have clean sheets on my bed as I have ascertained by personal examination and that is the chief thing.

Yr. Loving brother,
Stanley

STANLEY'S JOURNAL

Norwich. April 1, 1862. Twenty days of silence, but for this I am not to blame, for my trunk has only just arrived here, and this book was safely packed away in it. But I will commence my retrospect at once.

The storm continued on Friday, and in the afternoon of Saturday, I started with Patience and took Louisa to ride. We went to the Village for the mail, and thence to Uncle Hermon's. We found him and Aunt Harriet gone to Manchester and the girls alone. I had a sort of unpleasant feeling that I should never see any of them again, and they all seemed more or less to share it so that we did not have a very pleasant time.

Next day I went to Boston . . . [and] next day I staid at home, and the day after came again to Boston. It seems so strange to be at Beverly without seeing dear Grandfather. I cannot feel regret for him, but his vacant place and the remembrance of his peculiar ways and expressions still give me a pang I cannot conquer. Would to God I had at this moment the peace he has attained.

After staying some time at the Randall's, and Sunday at Newtonville, making a will, and doing some other business with Edwin, I started for Norwich to take private lessons of General Jackman while waiting for my appointment, which may be delayed three or four mos. Edwin says. I don't dare to think of ultimate failure.

I got here, as I said, a week ago today and, after some trouble, arranged to take my private lessons and to board

OLD NORWICH UNIVERSITY BUILDINGS
1862

with a Mrs. Doue who lives in a rickety brick house within gunshot of the "Norwich University" which consists of two great ugly factory like buildings (called North and South Barracks) standing within a level enclosure of some five or ten acres almost entirely destitute of trees.

The University contains about a hundred pupils, and is divided into a classical and a scientific department. It has a college charter, though it is chiefly, and indeed almost solely, a military school. The classics taught amounting to absolutely nothing at all.

There is a small village of some twenty houses or so near the "parade ground," a tavern, and a variety store. The whole is placed three quarters of a mile back from the Connecticut River, and is surrounded by high hills which limit the view to a mile or two in almost every direction. It will be pretty in summer I should judge, and in the vicinity there must be fine views.

I go in every day from ¼ to 1 to ¼ to 2 to recite to Gen. Jackman, and today he complimented me by saying I could command a company and carry it anywhere. I study until time to recite after which I return to my room, and read or write, or do something until the mail comes when I read the paper until suppertime. I shall study more now. For thus far, I have only gone as far as I could recite in an hour, which I could learn in 3 hours, but now I am going into Artillery and I take it I shall have to study that quite hard.

———

Norwich
April 1, 1862

My own dear Mother,

I have made another acquaintance in the person of Monsieur Balliard, Prof. of modern languages in the Norwich University. He is a typical Frenchman, small and wiry, with fierce black eyes and hair that stands "on end like quills upon the fretful porcupine. . . ." I can think of no one whom he resembles except that fiery little Garcon in *The Newcomes* who has "an hereditary hatred of *les*

Anglais" and whom poor Lord Kew pitches head over heels out the window.[7]

Despite the awe inspiring exterior of Mons. Balliard, he is at heart the most amiable and genial of good fellows. He plays on the piano in a manner which, at once, caused me to form the determination of cultivating his acquaintance. He is a very intelligent man and a perfect French gentleman and for my part I do not know why that is not giving him the highest possible praise as an acquaintance for their national courtesy and kindliness of manner make the French the most delightful of companions.

As for the place itself, Norwich may be best described as an enormous pig sty. Filth, nothing but filth, all over town owing to the fact that we are thawing out. I stay in the house all the time since it is a sheer impossibility to walk the street and the weather is too cold as yet for me to wear nothing but my swimming drawers and paddle round town.

Your loving son,
Stanley. Love to all.

STANLEY'S JOURNAL

Norwich, April 3rd. Night before last I staid as I intended with Gilbreth. In the evening at roll call the fellows tried to steal the drum, but Tutor Shattuck and Adjutant Kellogg were too much for them. A large kerosene lamp was brought out into the passage, so the fellows dared not raise a rumpus, reversing the old French proverb that "every man is a coward in the dark."

The following journal entry is one of the few times Stanley commented on his efforts to develop a skill in writing by actually writing.

---

7. Reference to William Makepeace Thackeray's nineteenth-century novel, *The Newcomes*.

STANLEY'S JOURNAL

April 6th, Sunday. Friday and Saturday both passed uneventfully. On the evenings I wrote and worked on my "Ransom of Calais"—I believe I might make something of that if I worked enough but blank verse is insufferably tedious without the melody of poetry or the facility of prose. Nevertheless, I wish to finish that if possible before I leave here. I can't take hold of "St. Malworth" somehow. I can't decide what his character is. It is all indistinct and uncertain. I can get particular scenes well enough but I can't support it yet. I must let that alone for I am determined not to spoil it.

Norwich
April 6, 1862

Dear Mother,

As for the town of Norwich, it is simply detestable at this season and as to the Norwichians, their only remarkable characteristic is that

"Their oaths been so great and so damnable
That it is grisly for to hear them swear!"

And I don't know as that is peculiar to them. However, as far as my limited experience has gone I think I know no body of individuals able to rival the "Cadets" in ingenuity—so far as that quality may be shown in inventing and employing new expletives. . . .

That cake you sent me was acceptable in the highest degree. Truth to tell, Mrs. Doue "has seen better days" and that she seems to consider a good reason for making all her boarders companions in misery in this her evil time. She does not keep a luxurious table.

The town or rather the Barracks are filled with sickness, 53 out of a hundred are sick! Diphtheria, measles, scarlet fever, everything under the sun except cholera and the small pox—As for me personally, I never was better in my life.

Your loving son,
Stanley

STANLEY'S JOURNAL

April 9, 1862. I find nothing very particular to write about these days. I spend much of my time in my own room and fence-drill and study my time away. Yesterday, however, when I went in to see Jackman, he told me he could do nothing more for me, that I had mastered the theory, and that all I wanted was practice. Consequently I do not recite to him today, but am waiting to hear from Edwin, to whom I wrote last evening.

Today Gilbreth was going up to Dutton's for some maple sugar and asked me to go with him. So we started off and had quite a pleasant four mile ride, passing Mr. Hazen's place on the way. I must go to see my Hanover bridge acquaintance. I met him on the way back from Hanover the other day and he gave me "a lift." Before many minutes were out, he had asked me a thousand questions, to some of which he got answers, to others evasions as it suited me. After he had got through, he proceeded to inform me of his views in regard to the status of our poor "Uncle Sam." He was all for a French despotism. His views were very singular for a country farmer and I must go up sometime and hear him talk.

April, 12, 1862. Yesterday, after I had studied my allowance, I finished the first act of the "Ransom," and in the evening went early to bed, to dream and dream, unsleeping, those delicious visions which are the chief happiness of youth.

They say, that as the years fly away they too spread their wings and come no more to make us half believe a Heaven may be possible for man. Ah well! Perhaps it is so—but if it be it is the saddest of the bitter griefs that are the bitter penalty of age! Health, strength and the buoyancy of early days I could lose, but to part from these sweet imaginings would be to be severed from my purest happiness. The actual world is harsh and sordid, mean and full of pain, but in the dreamy regions of fancy all is sunshine, love and joy—May the day be slow to come when the portals of that fairy Eden shall be closed to me! Pish!

Today I began "School for the Battalion" and toward noon who should come in to see me but my eccentric friend of Hanover bridge. He staid some time and cordially invited me to visit him, which I will do.

Norwich
April 13, 1862

Dear Mother,

Tout arrive en France, they say. Surely then, Norwich is the antipodes of France for nothing happens here. I live by the duly proportioned use of victuals and drink, and that is all I have to say about myself. . . .

Norwich, Vermont
20th day 4th mo.

Dear Mother,

Sunday has come once more and Sunday morning sees me, as is my custom, writing to my own dear mother.

The last few days have been a time of considerable anxiety here for the snow, which is now rapidly melting, has swollen all the streams in the neighborhood until many of them have overflowed their banks, swept away their bridges, inundated all the low land in their vicinity and spread terror and dismay throughout the entire Connecticut Valley.

The river itself is now higher than it has been for many years and it still is rising. Railroad communication between Boston and Norwich has been cut off by the destruction of the railroad bridges across the swollen stream and still further damage is feared. . . .

I, however, am not so badly off as many of the fellows who are prevented from going home by this unprecedented freshet. I know how to pity them for I well remember how I longed for vacations at Exeter and how disappointed

I used to be if anything delayed my return home even for a single train after the vacation had actually come. Well, they will have to bear it, I suppose. Though as to the proverbial "grinning," I see very little of it on the discontented faces around me. I am well and, in a certain sense contented though, of course, the "season of waiting" is as distasteful to me as to most persons but with exception of the uncertainty of my future everything else connected with my present condition is pleasant and satisfactory.

I begin already to perceive what I need to become a good and efficient officer and that is a great thing in itself. I am soon to begin a course of mathematics including Trigonometry, Analytical Geometry and last, but most assuredly not least, that terror of students, the Differential Calculus.

In addition to all this when next term commences I shall regularly drill with the "Cadets," as these blue coated gentry call themselves, twice a day once in Infantry and once in Artillery. So you see that my time will be fully occupied as long as I stay here which I most sincerely trust may not be more than two or three months at the utmost, "so mote it be!"

Love to Father, Willie and the Beverlais.

Yr loving son,
Stanley

Stanley showed a remarkable appreciation for the inherent goodness and honesty of individuals in this small town no matter how strange were their ideas or opposite were their beliefs to his. In his view, a carpenter who believes that the "railroads were spoken of in the Bible" was an "honest man."

STANLEY'S JOURNAL

April 25, 1862. Saturday I went to ride on Gibb's pony, as I intended to do every Saturday. It will only cost 50 cts.

a week. I shall do it as a part of my military education and it will be twice as cheap as a recitation to the Gen. By the way, in the evening I called to see him and had a nice chat about the men he has fitted off to the war.

Of course he has his vanity like most other men—just as Capt. Stevens, who mended the door in my room, has his. This devout one tried to convince me that railroads were spoken of in the bible because there is a prophecy to the effect that hills shall be made level and valleys filled which he says is fulfilled in "the gradings of the railroads!" The one man prides himself in his skill in the art of destroying the works of God, the other on his knowledge of one of the works of men. Both are honest, however, which not only makes their vanity pardonable but themselves respectable.

When I took my ride, I visited Mr. Hazen who introduced me to his nieces, and promised to introduce me to all his friends in town.

———

Norwich
April 26, 1862

Dear Ed,

I have made the acquaintance of a jolly old farmer by the name of Hazen who is really quite a character. He plays really artistically on the violin and entertains the most remarkable views of pretty nearly everything in general and of this war in particular. He gave me a ride from Hanover Bridge a week or two back and seemed quite to fall into friendship with me at first sight, to alter an old phrase. Since then he has called to see me. Invited me to his house today.

When I went there, he received me most cordially and addressed me pretty nearly as follows: "Mr. Abbot, you seem from all I can learn, candid." Wasn't he to tell me he had been asking questions about me? "A young man of a most exemplary character and I am happy to have made yr. acquaintance. I may truly say you have impressed me very favorably and, as I hear you intend making some stay in Norwich, I thought you might like to become acquainted

with some of its people. It would afford me great pleasure
to introduce you to many of my friends in the town if this
should be agreeable to you."

I was profuse in thanks, of course, and was amazingly
tickled both at his manner in making me the proposal and
at the proposal itself for the old gentleman knows the very
best people in town and there are really many educated
and refined people here (considering the size of the place)
and by his means I shall get into houses from which the
students are excluded on account of their "*notorieuse
black-guardianism*" as Prof. Balliard styled it to me the
other day.

I declare I have been the luckiest fellow here in
Norwich. I have made lots of friends from Prof. J[ackman]
down. I surely must be in luck! 'Twas a clever thing in the
old gentleman to make the offer, wasn't it? I shall think well
of fiddlers ever after for his sake. In fact I believe my audible
admiration of his musical performances is the true secret of
the affair. Flattered vanity is apt to make us good natured.

Brother Stanley

In the following letter, Stanley discloses to Frank his attention to "the preparation which sometime may teach me to
write." After Stanley's death, Edwin sheds more light on this
preparation. "I now have many manuscripts of his.—stories,
plays, songs and the like—and it may be that among them there
is something worth preservation. For this purpose, he went to
college carefully guarding from almost everyone his secret. This
was his ulterior design in entering the Regular Army."[8] Only a
folder of poems and a play have so far been found.

Norwich
May 3, 1862

My own dearest Brother [Frank],

I feel just like talking with you, I should want the
lamps put out and you and I to be seated in a nice

---

8. Abbot, "Edward Stanley Abbot," 432.

comfortable lounge. You should have your arm round my waist and I would lay mine on your shoulder and rest my head upon it and then we should have a lazy chat together broken by long pauses and filled with all sorts of nothings such as only happy people think of but, dear me, there are rivers and towns and states between us and this wish, like most others, cannot be gratified and I must grin and bear my disappointment or bear it without groaning, just as I please. Well, I'll write to you.

I don't suppose you are at all vexed with me for not having written to you. You know that I love you dearly. You know that you are more deep in my confidence than anybody in the whole world and you don't think my affection is weak or capricious or forgetful because I have not told you of it for so long. . . .

The fact is letters are a humbug in general. One sits down with lots of ideas and in covering the pages he does not express or imply one of them. It is just as it is in writing a poem or a story. One can't daguerreotype the original conception at all and so letters and poems and stories all disappoint the author of them. . . .

The impulse to write to you is the only reason why I should do so. I feel the impulse now, not that I have any news to tell or anything of the sort. This desire, like every other, has no cause except itself and I gratify it as I do my appetite for food or music or poetry, simply because I feel it.

I am much changed since I saw you pass behind Dane Hall just after you had said "watch and pray."[9] My face and mind and thoughts all are changed. The major part of my life seems crammed between that time and this for feelings, not years, make life and I have felt much since I watched you pass under the trees of the dear old college yard. I am a good deal less of a boy, something more of a man.

The childish ambition I cherished there has deepened and become the aim of my life, I have produced and

9. Dane Hall is on the Harvard Yard. The reference is to their parting, when Frank left Harvard for the Meadville seminary.

destroyed ever so much "veal" and I still keep on at leisure moments the preparation which sometime may teach me to write. You can't tell how perfectly sure I feel that I have neither overestimated nor mistaken myself. Sometimes I think I am a very vain sort of coxcomb to feel so calm and confident about the matter and yet I cannot teach myself to distrust. . . .

I declare I can't explain the absorbing interest I take in this war. I used rather to pride myself as being firm on my toddles both literally and figuratively but, I own, this enthusiasm about the war has entirely taken me off my feet and what's more I see no prospect of regaining my balance while the rebellion continues. Yet somehow the new object chimes in with the old and "going for a soldier" and going "for to be" a writer are connected in my mind in a most incomprehensible manner.

> Goodbye, dear old boy,
> Stanley

Norwich
May 8, 1862

Dear Mother,

Everything in Norwich remains in status quo except that I have made a new friend. Mons. Chaumier, the French Professor and successor of our fiery garcon, Balliard. He and I have suddenly struck up quite an acquaintance. He is intelligent. Consequently he finds himself almost wholly without companions in this Headquarters of Stupidity, Norwich. This being the case, he seeks my company a very great deal which is flattering to my vanity since, as I before said, he is bright and able. He plays chess well and occasionally we try a game to the satisfaction of both. This afternoon I am going to take a walk with him up a beautiful country road that follows a laughing rivulet for more than a mile. It is so pretty that I often wish I could have you here to enjoy it with me.

I only wish you could be a little happier in Beverly. My heart aches when I think of your situation now, Henry in the field and all your other children except dear little Pug[10] parted from you and, well, Em will soon be at home and then you will have other cause than misery to love her company.

Yr. own loving son,
Stanley

STANLEY'S JOURNAL

Friday, May 9. Quite a long gap in my journal—and that only corresponds to the state of my "life romance," in that little has occurred worth recording since I last wrote here. I have been to call on several families in company with ye eccentric Mynheir Hazen, to wit, Capt. Partridge, a fat and rubicund secessionist, Mr. Hazen, the orthodox minister, Mrs. Wright and her daughter whose sole charm lies I believe in a prospective fortune of 20,000 or more dollars. With the exception of these calls, I have been in my room the whole 19 days of my silence, with the exception of my daily visits to the mail.

Norwich
May 14, 1862

Dear Edwin,

I have not seen Jackman yet as I got your letter only Saturday and I could not call on Sunday. Of course, I will see him today, however, and find out what he thinks under the circumstances I had better do. You ask what plan I have formed and I answer, none at all. I am in a complete quandary. I don't know where I can be better situated in every respect to carry out my plans than I am here and yet Prof. J[ackman] tells me it is wasting time to stay here. I will see him again and have a good long talk with him for

---

10. Brother Willie.

he is very friendly and will give me the best advice he can
I am sure.

Yr. Loving bro.
Stanley

———— ⎯⎯ ————

Norwich
May 15, 1862

Dear Edwin,

I am beginning to get really discouraged. During
vacation, I studied a good deal and took little exercise, I
suppose, and the consequence is that my head troubles
me again. Now what am I to do? I can't study more than
two or three hours every day no matter how well I feel
without bringing on the old tight feeling. For the past few
days I have given up my mathematics and drill and get
along in artillery etc. and I felt so nicely that this morning
I thought I would try a little analytic. I commenced at 9
and now it is not eleven and my head aches. What shall
I do with myself? Is this going to haunt me as long as I
live? I thought a winter's rest had cured the whole trouble
and you can't tell how disheartening it is to find myself
mistaken.

Stanley

———— ⎯⎯ ————

Norwich
May 25, 1862

Dear Mother,

I no longer live in a pigsty. Norwich is most beautiful.
Within the last three days the bare, unsightly trees have
put on the verdure of the soft spring foliage. The grass and
flowers have risen from their graves, and everything, from
the twittering robin that is building his nest beneath my
window to the emerald hills beyond the churchyard, bear
witness that the ideal May is really come.

To tell the truth I believe our staid old Mother Earth is flirting with that ardent lover of hers, Dan Phoebus[11] and that this sudden suffusion of richest green is her way of blushing at the warm glances of the loving sun!

People talk of the beauties of Summer and Fall and Winter, and we sometimes persuade ourselves that we like all of those seasons best of all the year, but we never think so when the Spring is with us. Then we know it must be always spring in Heaven. I declare I think the older I grow the more I love natural beauty. I never was so delighted in my life as I am now to see every dead thing live once more in the fresh birth time of the year.

> Yr. loving son,
> Stanley

Norwich
May 30, 1862

Dear Edwin,

Now I have only to say that I wish you would feel perfectly at rest about me. I shall do precisely as you say throughout in this matter. I shan't play Stanton[12] and interfere with the general's plans! Of course from time to time I shall ask questions, make suggestions etc. and if you think it best to ride over them rough shod don't feel uneasy lest I may feel injured.

Don't waste time in allaying an irritation I shan't feel. Such folly on my part is among the things of the past. Nothing on earth could shake my absolute confidence in your brotherly love for me and in your unselfish eagerness to aid me.

In your letters I see now and then a timidity in opposing me, a sort of deprecatory tone, of which probably you may be unconscious, yet which causes me more

---

11. Dan is a title of honor, generally used by the poets. Phoebus is the sun god of antiquity.
12. Secretary of War, Edwin M. Stanton.

shame and sorrow than I can tell, for I know it springs from a want of confidence in me, that I myself am to blame for.

It is my dearest hope almost that one day I may atone for the errors and weaknesses of the past and thus earn the confidence of my dearest brother which I would purchase at I know not what sacrifice. I know you cannot give it to me now. Such things are not gifts and prizes.

Your loving brother,
Stanley

STANLEY'S JOURNAL

June 1, 1862. It is long since I have written here. 22 days full of expectation and anxiety. Now the expectation has been disappointed but in its grave I cannot bury my anxiety. Edwin some time ago wrote me that he had probably succeeded in getting me a commission in Major Copeland's Regt.[13] After much correspondence he sent me word yesterday that he had failed, that Major Copeland was not going to raise a Regt., and that my chance has gone. Oh! The sickening disappointments that men breathe with the air that gives life! I would so like to fall asleep and escape it all! Everything has gone on as usual. I drill at six in the morning and at four in the afternoon. All the rest of the time nothing happens and I am sick and weary.

Norwich
June 1, 1862

Dear Mother,

June 1, 1862. Everything goes on the accustomed way. No variety. No change of any sort. The only "event" that has befallen me for weeks is yesterday's ascent of Mt. Ascutney. This makes a pretty jaunt since it is three miles from base to top and a precious poor path at that. I was not more than four or five hours on the mountain for my

---

13. This was a volunteer regiment rumored to be forming in Massachusetts.

companion, a fellow by the name of Kellogg, did not wish to spend the night there as I myself did. So we came down in the afternoon and slept respectably in our beds. The view from the summit, like all mountain views, is rather novel than beautiful. It was nothing but a "colored bird's eye map" on a large scale.

However, Ascutney has two advantages over most mountains, i.e., a vicinity to Connecticut [River] and the fact that the country is cultivated on all sides up to its very base. There too Ascutney is much higher than any surrounding elevation. For all this region is made up of a succession of low rolling hills. Way off to the west, so faint and dim as to seem hardly the remembrance of mountains, were to be seen three or four peaks of the Green Mountains while in the east was a lofty range which I take to be Monadnock.

Altogether I am very glad I made the excursion. Windsor [Vermont], in which Ascutney is situated, is a beautiful town, especially the Northern part. The houses are mostly fine and the streets are shaded by beautiful elms.

> Yr. loving son,
> Stanley

> Norwich
> June 4, 1862

Dear Edwin,

Of course your letter was very full of sadness to me but one is not worthy to fight Secessionists who cannot conquer the blues. So I beg to be cheerful. My motive in writing you tonight is this. Capt. Sweet of the 17th Regular Infantry is at Lebanon (close by Norwich) recruiting, and he has it nearly in his power to procure five or six Lieutenancies in his Regiment for those whom he thinks qualified. I met him today in Norwich and he told me of this chance.

The 17th is commanded by Col. Greene, brother of Greene in the Senior Class [at Harvard] and son of the ex-Mayor of Cambridge. Can you give me a lift in this matter? Perhaps you know Col. Greene, or someone who can influence him by a letter. If so can I count on your aid?

Of course I know I can if you approve my conduct and I am most anxious that you should approve what I have done. It does seem somewhat like taking a case out of one's lawyer's hands, but I did what I thought was best. It would not pay to linger on in the hope of an Artillery commission months hence if I can get an Infantry one now. Please write soon if only a line to say you don't blame me.

> Yours in a pitiable state of
> bewilderment and anxiety,
> Stanley

> Boston
> June 5, 1862

Dear Stanley,

I have just taken your letter from the office. I can only write a word to say that you did just right, and I am heartily glad. Say to Capt. Sweet that Col. Greene knows your Brother Henry well and you can refer to Henry.

> In much haste,
> your affec. brother,
> Edwin

STANLEY'S JOURNAL

June 12, 1862. A week ago today Rice and myself went to Lebanon where I saw Capt. Sweet. He seemed, alone perhaps, very hopeful of getting me a commission, and was very kind and cordial. After some stay at Lebanon, we drove back along the river side through Hanover to Norwich, enjoying much our morning excursion in so pleasant a country as is the Connecticut Valley. The river and the straggling line of hills on either side make an infinite variety of charming scenes even in the short distance we traveled, hardly five miles.

Next day I got a letter from Edwin approving heartily all I had done, which relieved me from a very uncomfortable doubt. Saturday morning I was obliged once more to see Capt. Sweet about a letter he wanted from me, so I rode down to Lebanon on horseback, a jaunt I shall probably repeat the day after tomorrow. I did not find him, since he was gone to St. Johnsbury on recruiting business. . . . However, the ride in itself was a great pleasure for I had a very spirited little mare that was as glad to go as I was to have her. I kept on a hard gallop the whole way.

Norwich, Vermont
June 15, 1862

Dear Mother,

This week I have seen the most ludicrous of all possible sights and my sides are sore with laughing. I have seen enthusiasm, in the object of which I did not sympathize. Well, I'll explain. Dartmouth College is situated in Hanover just opposite the Norwich University and on the opposite side of the river. Between the students of the former and the Cadets of the latter institution there has always been hostility as bitter as the famous feud of the Camerons and Assynts.[14] Nothing has been able to conquer this hatred. Temporary truces have but led to more remorseless wars. Fights without number have crystallized the animosities of the combatants and nothing but annihilation can extinguish their cherished anger.

Such being the state of feeling in the two colleges, it was suddenly announced the other day that the "Darties"

---

14. Stanley was probably referring to Clan Cameron and Clan Mack-intosh, the Scottish Highland clans who famously had a feud that lasted over 300 years. http://en.wikipedia.org/wiki/Clan_Cameron. Last updated May 6, 2012.

were going to send off a company of 3 mos. volunteers in the 2d Rhode Island Cavalry. A 20 inch shell would not have occasioned half the excitement in Norwich had it fallen into the centre of the So. Barracks. The Cadets were fired! What, should those miserable Darties prove themselves more bellicose than the warlike and brass buttoned Cadets? Forbid it, Pompons and Shoulder Straps! A meeting is convened. It is enthusiastically attended, patriotic resolutions are passed. It is voted to enlist in the 3 mos. Cavalry in the midst of deafening cheers and the wildest of hurrahs! 30 to 40 Cadets will go and the honor of Norwich is served!

Now all this is contemptible for the reason that the patriotism is all sham. These fellows want to go off on a "bender" for 3 mos. That is all. Many of them publicly say that they enlist because they know it to be impossible to drill the company sufficiently in 3 mos. to make it possible that they shall be carried face to face with the enemy! Is not that shameful? A man becoming a soldier only because he can never use the sword he wears! They will be stationed at Washington to carry messages and to patrol the streets. And for this these fools are willing to sacrifice one twelfth of their college course![15] It is not a similar folly I have committed. I am to be a soldier permanently, they but for a span of time.

Stanley

STANLEY'S JOURNAL

June 13, 1862. [Following a description of the enlistment plans described in the letter to his mother above.] Alas! What a contemptible thing is enthusiasm to one who does not sympathize in its object! I hope my enthusiasm is wiser and more manly but then one can have more impartial judges than oneself. Oh for a measure to measure things

---

15. This anecdote may explain why 100 percent of Norwich University's 1862 Senior class enlisted in the army!

by! What would I not give to know whether I am an ass or a genius, a coward or a hero, a scoundrel or a saint?

———

Norwich
June 22, 1862

Dear Mother,

There are one or two things you say, however, which make me a little uneasy. You speak of my possible success in getting an appointment as a thing to be dreaded. It is distressing to me to think that tidings which in spite of myself must keep me forever so long in a perfect fever of joy must also inflict pain upon my own dear Mother. I cannot go back now and every feeling of preference urges me to keep on and I do hope you will spare yourself and me the exquisite pain we both must suffer if you continue to feel on the subject as you did when it was first broached to you.

Love to all from yr. loving son,
Stanley

While the following letter of recommendation must have arrived too late to be used since it remains in the Abbot Archives, it still reflects favorably on Stanley and his family. A. P. Peabody was Preacher to the University and Plummer Professor of Christian Morals.[16] As such he must have known Stanley, Edwin, and probably, Hale, personally.

Mr. Edward Stanley Abbot was for more than a year, & till obliged to withdraw by the condition of his health, a member of Harvard College. During his membership he was exemplary in conduct, faithful and successful as a scholar manifesting mental ability & traits of moral excellence which secured for him the cordial respect, esteem and confidence of the College Faculty. Independently of his college life, I am also acquainted with his domestic position, relations and character, & they are

---

16. *The Harvard Crimson*, March 19, 1891.

such as to entitle him to the highest regard, and to give the best possible guarantee for his diligence, probity & fidelity in any trust that may devolve upon him.

A.P. Peabody, Acting President,
Harvard University
Cambridge, June 26, 1862

CHAPTER 10

NOT A DAMNED FOOL
JULY, 1862–DECEMBER, 1862

Let us have faith that right makes might, and in that faith,
let us, to the end, dare to do our duty as we understand it.
—ABRAHAM LINCOLN, Cooper Union Speech
February 27, 1860

Stanley was on the road to success at last. On July 1, 1862, he enlisted at Ft. Preble, Portland Harbor, Maine as a Private in the 17th Regiment, United States Infantry determined to earn his commission by hard work augmented by lobbying on his behalf by Henry and Edwin. Diligence in pursuit of the goal rapidly earned an appointment as Second Lieutenant on November 10, 1862. Following a last visit at home, Stanley led a group of thirty-eight recruits to Virginia without losing a one.

> Ft. Preble,
> Portland Harbor, Maine
> July 6, 1862

Dear Mother,
I have just got back to the Fort and am as busy as busy can be, so I can only say a few words. I think I shall take my chance here and give up all attempts in other quarters,
> Goodbye, Yr. loving son,
> Stanley

Ft. Preble
July 14, 1862

Dear Edwin,

I have been appointed Lance Corporal[1] and have served first as Corporal and afterwards as Sergeant of the Guard, a responsible position. . . . I have passed my trial in drilling. . . . Of course I can tell nothing of my prospects. They are still in the clouds. I can only patiently wait until those clouds descend in gentle showers on my shoulders and cause to spring up thereon a couple of shoulder straps which will be a most welcome harvest.

It seems almost impossible, however, when I see what a position I occupy to believe that success is to await me. It is said that difficulties become smaller as one approaches them. Well it may be so but certainly in this case what appeared insignificant almost at first and at a distance looms up with [greater] magnitude now and close at hand. I have not lost heart at all. I shall give myself a fair chance but I much fear that merit alone, even were it mine, will not settle the matter and I much fear that appointments from civilian life will be made to destroy my only possible approach to the Eden of "Officer's Quarters."

Yr. Loving brother,
Stanley

Ft. Preble
August 1, 1862

Dear Edwin,

I am now Lance Corporal although I act in the capacity of Sergeant. I think it not improbable that I may be appointed Lance Sergeant quite soon, as they have thrown a great deal of responsibility upon me lately, and this morning have put me into the largest and most disorderly

---

1. A Lance Corporal is typically a noncommissioned officer of the lowest rank.

room in the Garrison to have complete control over it and to be responsible for its good order, an unpleasant duty to be sure but one that is going to be done up in good shape as one stupid ass of an Irishman found out to his cost this morning. I have had my first skirmish with insubordination and have achieved a complete triumph. The fellow would not clean up his bunk when I ordered him to do so. I succeeded in persuading him to do it, however, after some little time. . . .

It is a bad thing about my present life that the evenings are wholly annihilated so that I have no time that I can call my own, except Sunday afternoon, and that period of leisure is usually broken in upon by so many little things that even that is lost to me. Now you really must make allowances for I really am very busy and I have not got fairly harnessed yet.

Col. Greene told me day before yesterday that he had no doubt but that I should get my commission and that I was doing very well indeed. He said that in a short time I would be attached to a company. This is precisely what I want. If I am attached, it will certainly be as Sergeant and once in the field I think I can trust myself to push myself.

You must not be hurt at my long silence. In honest truth, I take the first opportunity of writing. I have been put in charge of nearly 40 new recruits and they take every moment of my time from morning till night. I have to show them everything, even how to fold their blankets and black their shoes.

Love to all,
Stanley

Ft. Preble
August 31, 1862

Dear Mother,

I am well and so busy. You would hardly know me now, I fancy. My hair is all but shaved . . . and brass

effects a marvelous change in my personal appearance.
I can assure you I make quite a spruce looking soldier.
My equipment is clean as any in the Fort and Cap. Chase
told me the other day that my musket was kept in "[good]
order." No small compliment let me tell you, from a man
so particular as this same Capt. Chase.

My dress coat, I sorrow to say, is rather shabby in
consequence of an absurd piece of folly. The other evening
it blew nearly a tempest here and the squall came on so
quickly that they did not have time to lower the flag, which
caught round the flag pole and flapped about in a most
furious fashion. A man was sent up to disentangle it, but
when he was half way up his heart failed and he came
down the quivering pole faster than he went up. As no one
else seemed inclined to make a second attempt, I thought I
would try and see what Harvard Gymnasium had affected
for me. So I climbed up and cleared the flag; at the same
time spoiled my nice coat by rubbing off the whitewash
upon it, which was disgusting.

Love to all,
from Stanley

While in Portland, Stanley renewed his acquaintance with
Cousin Martha Trask Steele, known as Mattie. "Addie" must
have been a childhood variant of "Mattie." The succeeding
chapters contain Stanley's letters to Mattie while he was on
bivouac in Virginia.

October 23, 1862

Dear Frank,

You know all about my old adoration of Addie. Now I
want to ask you if you don't think this is strange. I know
as well as any one exactly what she is. She is neither very
intelligent, nor very pretty, nor very good. If we should ever
be married, we should be miserable, I don't doubt. She
wouldn't care what I should write, not a brass farthing.

We have absolutely nothing in common except a love
of music and yet, will you believe it, I have just the same

MARTHA TRASK STEELE
1839–1932

love for her I have had ever since I was eight years old! Don't you think this is a curious case? I never heard of such a one.

I know all about her faults and how perfectly unsuited she is to me and I to her and yet all this has nothing to do with my feelings. I am determined that I won't make a fool of myself. I think there is no danger of that at all.

I surely tell you this to ask what the deuce is the explanation of it. 'Tis perfectly incomprehensible to me and yet the fact is, as I have stated, I tingle all over when I hear her voice or touch her hand just as I did when I used to write sonnets in her praise and thought her the standard to measure beauty by.

Yes, although I fully appreciate her snub nose and ugly chin and cat's eyes and faulty teeth . . . and platitude[s] and bad spelling! Is not this well calculated to excite wonders? This is rather jocose and perhaps you won't believe that it is so but literally it is. Never was a fellow more completely caught than I. I am more than head over heels in love and fathoms deep. Haven't seen the surface since I was nine!

Stanley

Anxious to move on from his life as an enlisted man, Stanley intensified his efforts to obtain a commission.

November 4, 1862

Dear Edwin,

Last night I got a letter . . . which induced me to see Col. Greene on the business of my commission. He complimented me highly on my progress, said he was perfectly satisfied with me and that he had only been waiting for a favorable opportunity to recommend me. He then said that, as my brother was in Washington, he would recommend me at once for a commission and told me to pile on all the influence I could bring to bear in any way to back it up. Henry wants all the letters of recommendation before Saturday or by Saturday certainly. An effort must be made Monday the 10th. Col. Greene's official recommendation will be at Washington by then. Henry says any new letters you can get will be of use.

Yr. Loving brother,
Stanley

—∞∞∞—

Ft. Preble
November 5, 1862

My own dear Brother [Edwin],

You can't tell how immensely I was relieved when I got your note. I had so feared you had not yet returned from Philadelphia. I enclose Henry's letter which you may like to see and then it saves me from making an abstract. Oh this laziness! I really begin to have hopes. I have not yet outgrown my boyish belief in your invincibility, and feel safe when I know that you are fighting my battles, and then that phrase "strong political influence" is so delightfully lawyer-like and indefinite. . . .

Through all the chaos of my religious views there is one belief that grows stronger and stronger every day, that God is good and that he holds me in the hollow of his hand. Don't mistake me, I am not creedish, not even a Christian, but I have learned to scorn no religion and to believe in God. I am contented to remain so, for I feel happier and more stable in mind than ever before in my whole life. Is there anything that can make a man so happy as to think that he possesses within himself the power to endure misfortune? I believe you thoroughly when you say that God alone can give us that power. That is all my religion, all the religion I shall ever have I honestly think.

Love to all. Yr. Loving brother,
Stanley

Stanley was granted leave to spend his twenty-first birthday on October 22 at home in Beverly. During this leave, he signed

EDWARD STANLEY ABBOT
SOLDIER
NOVEMBER, 1862

a will whose first priority was to pay any remaining debt owed to Edwin and Henry for amounts advanced "to assist me to obtain a liberal education and to start in my profession."

>Portland, Maine
>November 20, 1862

Dear Edwin,

I have just got fairly settled in my new capacity as absolutely a man with nothing to do, and to tell the truth I do not find the position destitute of charms. I arrived in due time (as my box did not) and reported myself to the Col. Apparently much to his surprise since he had not expected me for ever so many days as he informed me to my infinite disgust. I reminded him of his caution to me to be back by Wednesday. At which he smiled and his manner said "My youthful Lieutenant, you are jolly green."[2] He then proceeded to inform me that I positively was of no importance and might amuse myself for the next week or so in Portland. So I incontinently left and took lodgings at a Mrs. Baker's, 26 Free St. where I am now domiciled. In a short time I am to forage for recruits in the volunteer camps in Mass. and in a month or so I shall have the delightful task of carrying all the deserters and hard nuts he (Col. G[reene]) can scrape together to the aid of their grateful and suffering country. Ecstatic all this! Isn't it?

>Happily and idly, happily because idly,
>Yr. loving brother,
>Stanley

STANLEY'S JOURNAL

November 24, 1862. [Ft. Preble, Portland] A five month's silence—In these 150 days I have accomplished all that my personal ambition asked for myself. Strange that I

---

2. The commission was effective on November 10, 1862.

have attained everything I hoped to acquire in fifteen years
in one third as many months!

I am a commissioned officer in the Regular Army of
the United States. My income will be good and sufficient.
I need no more anxiety about my affairs. At twenty-one,
I have now absolute independence—henceforth, I can
educate myself to write—to write—to be happy.

I enlisted on the first of July at Fort Preble, Portland
Harbor, Me. and gradually rose from the position of a
private to be Lance Corporal, Acting Sergeant, full Sergeant
and 2nd Lieutenant. It cost me four months and ten days to
[regain the] position of a gentleman which I had voluntarily
resigned—a few days, an infinity of time, for life is emotion,
and the succession of light and darkness men call time.
Well this shall serve as a prelude. I will write tomorrow.

December 14, 1862. Well it is six months today since
my story was really broken off, and, since it would be
impossible to write a particular account of each day, I will
just record those things about which I have thought most
during the past half year and, in the first place, about
military matters. I enlisted under Lieut. Edward Collins,
who has charge of the Unattached Recruits at Fort Preble,
in accordance with the advice of Col. Greene whom I
consulted upon the step and to whom I brought many
letters of recommendation. He said, when I asked him for
his advice, "Well, Mr. Abbot, I don't know whether you are
a damned fool or not. If you are, you had best not enlist.
If you are not, you are sure of your commission in time."
This being the case, I enlisted, and the result, according to
Greene, has proved that I am not "a damned fool." That is
satisfactory.

For four months I was gradually working my way along.
At first, I and Smith, Buell, and Babbitt, 3 fellows who had
also been at Norwich, lived together in a room at the "Buck
Barracks" and a precious poor time we had of it. We all
hated three persons in the room and nobody hated himself.
Consequence was that I broke up the establishment and
shortly after went over to take charge of the largest room

in all the Barracks with from twenty to thirty men in it. And here I stayed until very near the time of my promotion to a Lieutenancy. At first, all was confusion but, at last, things settled themselves.

A short time after this, Smith and Babbitt went off to join the 1st Battalion in the field. After this, I got along better. I was then third in command of the "Permanent Party." Holmes, a Sergeant, was sick, and his place was supplied by Corporal Nixon. At last this person also left to join Co. A. 2nd Battalion and that left me Act. Ord. Sergeant. I was soon after promoted to be full Sergeant and Holmes and I divided the responsibility. I drilled the men constantly and finally the Col. sent for me one day and told me he would recommend me on the first opportunity. Shortly after this I went home to pass my birthday. I had a nice talk with Edwin about my situation and we decided to ask Henry to make an effort for my appointment. I was to get a letter from Col. Greene and Henry was to push it.

When I got back to the Fort, I got the letter I wished for from Col. Greene together with an official recommendation. As he gave me these letters, he told me that ever since I had been at the Fort my conduct had been perfectly satisfactory, that I had proved myself able to make a good officer, that if I failed now not to be discouraged, and that he would never leave the matter until I had my commission. Well, I sent the letters on and in three or four days my appointment as 2nd Lieutenant came back. Its date was Nov. 10, 1862.

That afternoon we stayed at the Webster's until the coach came for me which was to separate mother and child, perhaps forever.[3] My poor Mother could not say much except "God bless you" and then I ran into the coach.

These partings are bitter! Well! When I got back to Portland, I boarded in town and drove over to report myself

---

3. This afternoon was, in fact, the last time Stanley and his mother saw each other.

every morning at the Fort.[4] In the evening I would either go up to Mr. Boyd's where my cousins Julia and Charlie Abbot are staying or I would go to see Mattie Steele.[5] Ah! What shall I say now? Mattie Steele, she is charming, so bright and witty—so pretty, so petite in her ways, so coquettish without coquetry. I went as often as I dared to see and talk with her. We are great friends, and I am going to write to her. In fact I have already. She is added to my list of friends which embraces now only Mr. Randall and Miss Belinda,[6] Chaumier, Gove and Mattie Steele. The day I came away I went to the house and prevailed upon her to ride over to the Fort with me. It was the first sleigh ride of the season for both for the snow was only a day old. I will long remember that bright, cheerful ride through the glittering snow.

The frosty air made the blood tingle and we knew that I was to go away that evening. She likes me just as I like her and I know that she will always be right glad to hear good of me. She has a trust in me and moreover she has a respect for my brain. In fact she puts about the same estimate on me that I put on myself. Now all this may go to show that I am a vain ass and fond of flattery. And upon my soul I am not prepared to say there is not a great deal of truth in that way of looking at the matter.

Now I certainly believe that I have a talent for writing. I actually think that if I live to be 35 years old I will have written the greatest and noblest novel that ever has been written but yet I submit that it is an open question as yet whether I am an ass or not. If I write the book, it is simply appreciated [by] myself. If I fail to do it, I will be content with a pair of long ears instead of a laurel crown. I think that is fair so I won't begin to call myself names yet.

---

4. See letter to Edwin from Stanley dated November 20, 1862 earlier in this chapter on page 154.
5. Distant cousins—Julia Abbot, age eight, and Charles Abbot, age ten— lived in Oxford, Maine according to the 1860 census, and must have been visiting in Portland at the time.
6. Miss Belinda Randall, sister of John Randall.

Now I think the reason I am so charmed with Mattie is that she somehow found out, soon after I first saw her, what my ambition was and then sympathized and believed with me. That may be flattery but it is also such help as angels give to men that are striving to do well.

This ambition of mine is not selfish at all. I have satisfied my personal ambition completely—I am a gentleman in station with a sufficient income to "keep the wolf from the door"—that is all I ever wanted for myself. I don't care for rank or money or anything of the sort. I will be a good officer and, as long as this war continues, I will use every power God has given me to make God's cause triumphant—But still all this is the preface to my real work, that is, simply putting coal into the engine.

If I am really going to do a great good in the world; if this machine which has to be fed and clothed was intended to effect a work that is to distinguish it from other lumps of clay that have walked about for a while and then tumbled down into the great bed of motionless clay once more; if in time I am to be a worker in God's vineyard; I must do my work by writing. I know this. I am sure of it. If I live and do not accomplish it, I shall have buried my talent.

On Monday, December 7, 1862, Stanley, along with thirty-eight recruits, took a ferry to the main Portland docks and boarded there a boat for the overnight voyage from Ft. Preble, Portland Harbor, Maine to Boston, Massachusetts. He had time for a brief visit with Edwin before they took a train to Providence, Rhode Island and boarded an overnight boat to New York City. After landing, he marched his troops to the Battery where a tugboat took them to Governors Island in New York Harbor. Following nine nights on Governors Island, they took a boat to Jersey City and the train to Washington. After a night of guard duty in the city, they boarded a river boat for the trip to Aquia Creek, an overland march to Falmouth, Virginia, and a camp near Potomac Creek. Resting from the long journey, Stanley had time to write in his journal and write letters again.

STANLEY'S JOURNAL

Camp near Potomac Creek. December 21, 1862.[7]
That afternoon, Dec. 7, I went to the Fort once more,
and marched away my squad. As I passed out the gate
where I had so often been on guard, the band struck up
"Dixie"[8] and so in the still evening 38 more men started
for Golgotha. It was dark when we crossed the ferry in two
large boats, and then the moon traced a path upon the
waters that seemed as bright as that I was to tread. Were
they equally treacherous? *Quien Sabe?* That night we spent
on the water. That night Mr. Boyd came to bid me goodbye
just before the boat started and, by him, I sent back love
to Julia and that darling little Charlie who was one of the
greatest charms of Portland to me.

Next morning Edwin met me on the Boston wharf,
and I went into town with him, and attended to some
business. In the evening I marched the squad to the Fall
River Station—Edwin leading the way walking by my side.
After the men were all safe in the [railroad] cars, Edwin and
I walked the platform together till the cars started.

Well, a weary ride in the cars, a hurrying scramble to
get on board the boat, a sound sleep in my state room,
a glimpse at Hells Gate and New York as it slumbered in
the grey mist of the morning, and the Steamer stopped. I
formed the men on the wharf and marched them to the
Battery, where we found a tug that carried us to Governor's
Island.

---

7. The December 21, 1862 journal entry, written after Stanley arrived in
   Virginia, covered various incidents that occurred after he joined the
   Army on July 1, 1862. It is split into three parts to maintain continuity
   in the story, even though the document parts are not in strict chronological order. Two parts are in this chapter and one part is in the next.
8. The song "Dixie" became the unofficial anthem of the Confederate
   States of America. http://en.wikipedia.org/wiki/Dixie. Last updated September 24, 2011.

Ft. Columbus
New York Harbor, New York
December 13, 1862

Dear Mattie,

Indubitably, I am blue myself. The reason of which
state of mind on my part is easily explained. I marched
into Fort Columbus with colors flying. I did not lose a man
on the way despite the predictions to the contrary of my
anxious friends at Fort Preble. I reported to Col. Loomis at
once, who received me very kindly and invited me to take
breakfast with him.

"Everything has gone on finely," I said to myself
applaudingly as I munched the Col's toast. "I will leave the
squad here and go right on by the evening train." While I
was lucubrating to myself after this fashion, mine host was
blandly expatiating to me on the beautiful situation of Fort
Columbus. To all of which praise I cordially agreed and
even went so far as to point out several advantages not
alluded to by the orator. Not that I really liked the boggy,
old mud hole, but I thought I would do the polite thing,
you know.

"Ah!" said the Colonel—"I'm glad you like the place
so well and I hope you will find no reason to alter your
opinion of it during your stay." "My stay," remarked I, "will
be so short that I will hardly have time to form my opinion,
much less to alter it" and to tell the truth I was pleased
with the sound of my remark and mentally patted myself
on the back and said "Clever boy"! "Eh! What," snapped
the Col., "What's that"? I explained to him that my orders
were to leave the detachment at Fort Columbus and
proceed at once to join my regt. in the field.

The Col. thoughtfully pulled a little promontory of
hair that bisects his bald pate something after the manner
of an augmented Indian scalp-lock and slowly drawled
out his words "I don't like," said he, "I don't at all like to
interfere with Col. J. Durrell Greene's orders but I—I am
afraid I shall have to." He gave his hateful [head] turned-
the-wrong way a final jerk and looked up at me. "Yes, Mr.
Abbot, you will have to stay here with the detachment, I'm

sorry to interfere but then you like the place, you know, and will enjoy staying here two or three weeks I am sure."[9]

The old wretch! He knew that no human being likes to live in a pig-sty. I wouldn't have cared so much if it hadn't been for that last jab about my "liking the place"! Catch me telling any more lies for anybody, that's all! Don't you remember what I grandiloquently remarked one evening about "worshiping truth"? Ah me! Would I had practiced as I preached. Henceforth my devotion shall be entire. I'll dive into the first well I find and draw Truth and myself up in the same bucket! I will, so help me. Patience to bear my imprisonment tangle! There is no tolerable aspect to the case at all!

If I had [not gotten] strung up by this miserable red tape, I would have seen the fun at Fredericksburg.[10] Now it will be all over before I get there. Oh Col. Loomis, Col. Loomis you've pulled that queue of yours long enough. What I wouldn't give if I could take my turn! Shouldn't it be a long pull, a strong pull and a pull altogether? Well, all I say is if I had only one pull, he should never have another, not even at the stubs!

Stanley

⁂

Ft. Columbus
December 14, 1862

My own dear Brother [Frank],

And now, dear old boy, goodbye. It has really been a good thing for me, this entering the army. I never would have respected myself at all had I not done so.

Yr. loving brother Stanley

---

9. In fact, Stanley stayed less than two weeks—from December 9 to December 18.

10. This journal entry was made on December 13 in the middle of the Battle of Fredericksburg which extended from December 11 to 15, 1862. http://en.wikipedia.org/wiki/Battle_of_Fredericksburg. Last updated October 28, 2011.

STANLEY'S JOURNAL

Camp near Potomac Creek. December 21, 1862. Col. Loomis paid me a compliment [at the time of my leaving Governors Island]. I went in soldier's clothes altered over, a stock and great boots, and I insisted upon his giving me a written order to stay upon the Island contrary to my original instructions. By these proceedings I supposed I had lost favor with him, but the Adjutant told me after I left his office, that the old Col. said, just after I left the room with my written order in my fist, which I had been fighting for ever since I came upon the Island, "That young man looks the soldier, acts the soldier, is the soldier, and only wants a little experience to become an ornament to the Service. He has the true snap and ring to him. You will hear of that young officer, Mr. Childs." Now perhaps I ought not to care a pin for a compliment like that, but it came from an old soldier of 53 years' experience in the Army, and human nature is weak, and I was quite elated at the circumstance.

Camp near
Potomac Creek, Virginia
December 21, 1862

Dear Mother,

I got safely through without losing a man and this, I can say without exaggeration, is very extraordinary good luck. They said at Fort Preble I could not get even to New York without losing at least five men. . . . Three or four days after [arrival at Governors Island] we were ordered off, myself and 4 or 5 other officers and some 300 men. . . .

After we landed at Jersey City from the red boat that carried us from the Island, we entered the [railroad] cars and rode all night and until 8 p.m the next day without seeing anything. I stayed with my men the whole time and did not lose one in consequence. The others more careless perhaps because more experienced slept soundly all night and each one lost two or three men.

When we got to Washington, all my men were put on Guard so that I was no longer responsible for them. This being the case . . . we stayed overnight in the city. . . .

Next morning we came down the Potomac to Aquia Creek and landed about sundown. Here we were fairly in Dixie and a miserable place it looked to be. Hills covered with stumps, frozen ditches for roads and not a fence to be seen, a dead horse here and there and scattered around apparently at haphazard were the dirty wedge-like "shelter tents" our army at present freezes under. That night, and a bitter cold one it was, we bivouacked on the bare ground, rather rough but we had a nice long march of 15 miles next morning to warm us up a bit. This brought us to Sykes' Headqtrs. where I now am.

> Your devoted son,
> Stanley

Chapter 11

Parting of the Roads
December, 1862–March, 1863

After complicated journeyings with many pauses, there had come months of monotonous life in a camp. He had had the belief that real war was a series of death struggles with small time in between for sleep and meals; but since his regiment had come to the field the army had done little but sit still and try to keep warm.

—Stephen Crane, *The Red Badge of Courage*

The long journey was over, not just the physical journey from Ft. Preble to northern Virginia, but the longer developmental journey from a boy of fifteen to a man of twenty-one. Now Stanley must deal with a wintry bivouac, with life as an Army Officer during a war, and with life as an adult.

General Robert E. Lee assumed command of the Army of Northern Virginia in June, 1862 and remained at the helm throughout the war. His leadership of the southern troops was overwhelmingly successful in northern Virginia until they ventured north to Gettysburg.

The Army of the Potomac's primary role was to defeat the Confederate Army of Northern Virginia, and thereby protect the nation's capital of Washington, D.C. In response to Lee's victories, President Lincoln churned through a number of generals searching for the one who could defeat such a formidable opponent. General George B. McClellan was popular with the troops, but failed to launch an offensive as requested by

President Lincoln. After his earlier triumphs, General Ambrose Burnside lost the Battle of Fredericksburg during the week before Stanley's arrival in northern Virginia; and rain and mud defeated his second initiative to capture Fredericksburg in mid-January, again after Stanley's arrival. General Joseph Hooker, after showing some leadership promise in his earlier endeavors, lost the Battle of Chancellorsville in which Stanley participated. General George Meade took over the Army of the Potomac just a few days before he triumphed with his troops in the Battle of Gettysburg.

Stanley noted in a letter to Mattie on January 29, 1863: "Oh it is not a pleasant thing to be one in an army that has failed. It is right hard to be cheerful sometimes. . . . It is a good thing to have an enthusiasm. . . . It enables one to say 'I believe the sun will shine upon our victory yet.'" Stanley never lost faith in the correctness of the North's cause nor in its ultimate success. Unfortunately, he did not survive long enough to enjoy the victory at Gettysburg.

Getting off the train in Washington, Stanley and his new recruits traveled forty-five miles south down the Potomac River past Mt. Vernon to Aquia Creek Landing, Virginia. The next day, he and his troops marched fifteen miles inland to Falmouth where over 100,000 men in the Army of the Potomac were settling into winter camp following their disastrous defeat across the river in Fredericksburg. The landscape was nearly bare of trees, which had been felled to use as firewood to heat the tents and provide kindling for cooking.

Fredericksburg occupied a position of strategic importance about halfway between the two capitals of Washington and Richmond. The capture of Fredericksburg by the North could lead to the capture of Richmond—so a successful defense of Fredericksburg by the South was essential.

The division's camp near Potomac Creek in Falmouth was between Henry House and Sykes Headquarters, and about four miles from the headquarters of the Army of the Potomac at Chatham House, which overlooked Fredericksburg across

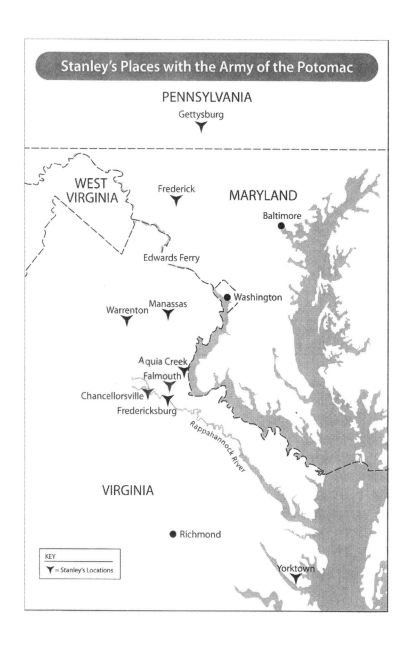

Stanley's Places with the Army of the Potomac

PENNSYLVANIA

Gettysburg

WEST VIRGINIA

Frederick

MARYLAND

Baltimore

Edwards Ferry

Warrenton Manassas

Washington

Aquia Creek

Falmouth

Chancellorsville

Fredericksburg

Rappahannock River

VIRGINIA

Richmond

KEY

= Stanley's Locations

Yorktown

the Rappahannock River.[1] As a consequence, Stanley used interchangeably the locations Falmouth, Henry House, Sykes Headquarters and Potomac Creek in his letters. Chancellorsville is another ten miles beyond downtown Fredericksburg.

During the first six months of 1863, Stanley mostly experienced the boredom of an army on bivouac with lots of time to write in his journal and correspond with the family. He ventured away from the camp only for the disastrous "mud march" in January (in the second failed attempt to attack Fredericksburg), a trip down the Potomac River to the Yorktown area at the entrance to the Chesapeake Bay for a brief time in April (purpose unknown), and the excitement of the Battle of Chancellorsville in early May.

STANLEY'S JOURNAL[2]

December 21, 1862. Camp near Potomac Creek, Virginia. That last snow ride with Mattie over and my life as an idler was gone forever. That "parting of the roads" will long be remembered, boyhood gone—manhood before me. Ah! It is not all pleasurable, this growth—one yearns to stay where the summons comes to go. "Perversity" Poe calls it. Perhaps it is the right name but at least it is a very gentle and loving feeling—not all bad.

When we reached Aquia Creek it was nearly dark. We marched through a large camp of Volunteers, and prepared to Bivouac for the night. I made the men stack arms, and unsling their knapsacks, and then sent them off to hunt for wood. It was not long before a dozen great fires were surrounded by a dozen rings of shivering soldiers for the night was bitterly cold. It was a picturesque sight, and I

---

1. Braddock's Second Brigade was camped in the center of Sykes Division. The site today is an open field on Crane's Corner Road (State Route 676), east of a power line crossing the road.
2. This is a continuation of the journal entry dated December 21, 1862 begun in the prior chapter.

could have enjoyed it but for the cold. As soon as the poor
fellows had swallowed their raw pork and hard tack, which
they generously shared with me who had eaten nothing
all day, they spread out their blankets and three or four
together tried to keep from freezing till morning. I know I
barely managed to do that. It was my first experience in the
"Sunny South," that wintry Bivouac!

Next morning we started early along the railroad to
Sykes headquarters.[3] My detachment, which was the best
drilled of the Party, formed the Rear Guard and I had the
pleasant duty of picking up the stragglers. The road wound
through hills that had once been covered with trees. Now
they were bare and cheerless. Not a fence have I seen
since I have been in Virginia. After a fatiguing march of 15
miles or so, we reached the Headquarters of Sykes passing
through several Cavalry encampments on our way.

Around us lies an army of probably 150,000 men. Each
member of which is suffering more physical pain probably
than persons ordinarily suffer for months together. It is
absolutely impossible to keep warm in these "Shelter Tents"
as they are inaptly called. The papers talk of the Army
being "comfortable" in these shrouds! How different are
these muddy, dirty wedges from the "tented fields" one
reads of!

My company has been detached from the Battalion
today, and assigned to Provost Guard duty near Gen. Sykes
headquarters. This everyone seems to think is a great piece
of good luck for me as it will keep me out of danger's way
in a great measure! I must confess to a feeling of utter
amazement at the manner in which I hear officers talking
of battles etc. They regard them as shunned in any way and
regard as fortunate and desirable any duty which will keep
them out of the way of bullets, no matter how disagreeable
that duty may be in itself. They are all, if one may believe
what they say, unconditional peace men opposed to the
prosecution of the war and in favor of the recognition of
the Southern Confederacy!

3. Major General George Sykes, Commander, 2nd Infantry Division, 5th
Corps, Army of the Potomac.

REPLICA OF SHELTER TENT
FALMOUTH, VIRGINIA

Shame on such men I say. I do not care how much they have suffered. No agony could excuse such opinions. They tell me I shall come to have the same. The prediction is childishly silly. My beliefs have nothing to do with the lowness of the Thermometer. It is only those who are babies that are influenced by the state of their cuticle. I trust goose flesh will never make me a secessionist.

After all, men of character and courage may be as rare among soldiers as they are in every other class of persons. Discipline and vanity may make these cowards stand fire, but they are not steadfast in mind. They are men who would be cowardly in their conduct of a dark night. Of this cheap material, victory is in part made. There are worthless persons whose loss is of no importance. These cowards must be used and turned to account. Would success could be bought with no more costly barter than the loss of these imbeciles!

And yet perhaps it is too much to expect that the majority of mankind shall see more than the shell of things. Thought is rare, thinkers few, and after all there can be no virtue outside of thought. Morality there can be, not virtue. Perhaps it is enough to require that the actions of men shall be right without examining into their motives.

Stanley arrived in Falmouth on December 21, less than a week after the end of the disastrous Battle of Fredericksburg. The experienced officers and men were discussing and reliving the battle. Stanley described what he heard to Emmie.

> Potomac Creek, Virginia
> December 22, 1862
>
> Dear [Sister] Em,
>
> We are encamped near Potomac Creek, about two miles from the [Rappahannock] river and the same distance from Fredericksburg. The army is resting after its movement of a week ago last Saturday—the most ill-judged and disastrous "piece of strategy" yet accomplished by this unfortunate army. The thing is easily understood.
>
> On the Southern side of the river is a narrow plain perhaps a mile or a mile and a quarter wide at the city of Fredericksburg though much narrower both above and below that place. This plain is perhaps two miles in length extending along the river side. Back of the plain and nearly parallel with the river is a ridge of low hills the summit of which was crowded with rebel batteries, and in the rear of this ridge there were still two others, all of them fortified. This was the battlefield or rather the slaughter pen.
>
> Our forces crossed at various points. All of them however were directly in front of this fortified ridge and

the most distant bridges were hardly more than two miles asunder. That is, the whole army was crowded into this narrow plain every foot of which was surrounded by rebel batteries.

All day Saturday Franklin, Hooker and Sumner pushed up their columns against this network of cannons in the vain hope of [breaking] some portion of the line which would have compelled the confederates to have abandoned the whole. But in order to make these attacks our troops had to pass over half a mile of open ground, without even a [tree] to cover them and exposed to the heaviest artillery and musketry fire ever known on this continent.

Franklin made a little progress which was however of no consequence as he only repelled the rebels who had rallied out of their works. The other two accomplished only a massacre of their own men. This day was bad enough but those who were there say it was nothing to the next day, Sunday.

The papers say the "army rested." It rested thus. Whole divisions and corps threw themselves at sunrise upon the muddy ground flat on their bellies and dared not turn over till night. All the time rebel sharp shooters were picking them off at their leisure.

Syke's Division lay all day within forty rods of the rebel lines and poor Capt. McLandberg of ours was shot through the head because he tried to roll himself over and raised his head a few inches. In so doing, not a man succeeded in getting to the rear during the whole day without being hit! This may give some idea of the accuracy of the rebel fire and of the proximity of our army to their lines.

It is probable that our loss, newspapers to the contrary notwithstanding, accounts to near 2800 killed, 8000 wounded and 8000 missing while that of the rebels no one here estimates at more than 500. . . . Such was the massacre of Fredericksburg. It is useless to call it a battle. . . .

One cannot estimate the harm of such blunders, blunders so heinous that they became crimes, by the number of killed and wounded. The effect of such things upon men's minds is so enervating and discouraging that the army becomes useless nearly. Brave officers were all unnerved that day and started for long after at a sudden noise, like a nervous girl.

I have not heard an officer, not a single officer, say that he thought we would ever be in Richmond, and I have heard at least thirty express the opposite opinion, and yet every one of these men said that before Fredericksburg he had believed in our final success inexplicitly. If this is the effect upon educated gentlemen, what must it be upon the men?

This affair is incalculably the greatest disaster of the war! Not that the actual loss is so crippling, though that is enormous, but this affair has taught men to profoundly distrust their government. The most absurd rumors were prevalent and are believed. Lincoln is crazy. He is a Secessionist. He meant to have destroyed the whole army. These are the rumors just now.

Last night the report came that McClellan had been restored. . . . It did my heart good to see men brighten up as they did and grow so enthusiastic over "little Mac." "Everything will go right now," said they. "We will be in Richmond before long now." And when the story was contradicted, it was sickening to see the old despondency return and the old distrust of those in authority along with it. If this army ever accomplishes anything, McClellan must lead it so everyone here believes and knows. Well, no one knows what is in store for us and I for one will keep hoping on.

You say you can't tell from my letter if I really like Mattie Steele or whether I am "fooling." I assure you I like her ever so much. I never struck up so sudden a friendship with anyone in my life as I have with her. We suit to a T for we are alike in nothing except our love of music so there is a chance to fight, therefore, to like each other. By the way what is her address? Do you know we are actually correspondents?

> Love to all from
> yr. own loving brother,
> Stanley

STANLEY'S JOURNAL

December 23, 1862. Nothing has happened since I last wrote here and I only write again because I have been looking over this book and am so disgusted with portions of it that I ache to castigate myself! It is singular how words fail to express ideas or rather how hard it is to make them do so.—Some of the very silliest of these pages stand for feelings that were not weak or silly at all. I feel that after all I owe myself an apology, dashing off these scraps as I do without any sort of revision, and at as fast a rate as my hand can move. I do think I appear more absurd than I really am.

December 26, 1862. [Christmas] night I crept into my bed and floated off into the fairyland of dreams and fancies until sleep threw its spell over me, as is my boyish and absurd want.

But suddenly any waking dreams seemed also to haunt my slumbers. The softest music sounded through the stillness of midnight and it was long before I could persuade myself that the strains were real and not imaginings. The band of the 2nd Infantry was playing Christmas anthems in the midst of a sleeping army.

The dreamy music, soft and low as a mother's prayer, floated over the camp and stole like a benediction into the half unconscious ears of the rude soldier around. First it was a dead march. Then a beautiful variation of "Gentle Annie"[4]; and last "Do they Miss me at Home?"[5] The

---

4. "Gentle Annie" is a song composed by Stephen Foster in 1856.
   Shall we never more behold thee?
   Never hear thy winning voice again,
   When the springtime comes, gentle Annie,
   When the wild flowers are scattered o'er the plain.
5. "Do they Miss me at Home?" is a song from 1852 that was familiar to both sides during the Civil War.
   Do they miss me at home, do they miss me?
   'Twould be an assurance most dear,
   To know that this moment some loved one
   Were saying, "I wish he were here."

effect was unequalled by anything I ever heard except that wonderful Death Chant which breaks in upon the mad drinkers of the poisoned wine in Lucretia Borgia.

That is the beauty of a soldier's life. There are some touches of purest romance occasionally breaking through the dull prose and bitter suffering. It is after all the only profession which rises above the common place. In it, beauty and effect are studied for and arrived at. Heroism and the most delicate refinement are necessary to the true soldier. It is that I believe which is so charming in the profession—that which renders it a fit place for a dreamer and a writer.

Ah yes, something has happened. I have heard from Mattie Steele. It was a delightful letter and then she wrote so quickly as soon as she knew my address. She is kind. She knows that poor fellows, away from all their friends, almost cry for joy at the sight of a letter, and so she honestly and kindly agreed to thus cheer me (as she would anyone who wanted cheering), and then kept her promise, which was kinder still.

———

Near Henry House, Virginia
December 28 1862

Dear Cousin Mattie,

Really, I was perfectly delighted at your prompt and honorable payment of your debt of correspondence. You ought to charge a premium for the good currency you returned for my depreciated (though more than appreciated) shinplaster. But you are generous; therefore, a terribly poor hand at business transactions. I am also glad that you have got rid of that tear you speak of. One mustn't cry for spilt milk. No, nor for spilt blood either. Though at times it may be hard not to do so as in the case of that wicked blunder of Fredericksburg. I call it a wicked blunder because sometimes it is a crime to be in error. Two weeks ago all the data of a correct judgment was at hand, yet it was not used, and in consequence there are three thousand new graves on the hillsides of Virginia. "Someone had blundered. . . ."

Hence! You say that you are glad I was not at Fredericksburg. Well, poorly as it may speak for my courage, I have altered my opinion since I knew about the affair and am glad too. I value my life and do not like to run the risk of absolutely throwing it away. Nay, even more, I am very far even now from "spoiling for a fight" and would be very glad if I might escape all danger of being in one, honorably that is. So I am afraid you wasted a little sympathy when you were "sorry for my disappointment" in not being in the late battle. Of course, I fear many things more but still it is indubitably that I fear cylindrical cannon balls. . . .

And now I have only to make my excuse for having written again so soon to you in dear old New England which I do love after all. I can hardly believe the fluttering in our hearts at the sight of a letter. A letter drives away the musky exhalations of camp immorality and is a breath of the sweet, clean New England air. It makes one remember that this is God's war although it seems to us these devils wage it. It strengthens and helps us and thus is why I write so quickly. I am as self-reliant as most, I think, but it is stultification to think that one does not need the help of others to do right. The best camp is an immoral, brutalizing place and I, for one, need many a helping lift from home. Will you not soon send a merry message of good will down into Golgotha? . . .

Would you believe it? So down hearted are men here that they smile at my folly when I say that I yet believe in our final success? I tell them, "Perhaps McClellan may return." "Ah, then indeed" say they with brightening faces. This army yearns after its only true leader. Severed from him it does not rebel, it only depends, which is almost worse. Our history will be loathsome to read if the present policy is consummated. Pray therefore, as I do, that McClellan and common sense and common honesty may return to us.

Once more, goodbye,
E.S.A.

Camp Sykes Division
Near Falmouth, Virginia
December 29, 1862

Dear Mother,

It is a beautiful afternoon, warm and sunny as an August day in the latitude of home and as I sit writing the gentle breeze comes puffing in through the open side of my tent and stirs my paper. The seventeenth is a portion of the 2d Brigade of Sykes' Division, Butterfield's (or rather Mead[e]'s) Corps and Hooker's Grand Division.

Consequently we lie two or three miles back of the river near the centre of the army, which is all concentrated within a distance of 5 or 6 miles. The country is hilly and in the valleys and on the summits of the lower elevations are clustered the encampments of the "Grand Army," par excellence. Our own camp is on a sort of plateau which gives just room for the 1st and 2d Brigades.

Perhaps it will give you a better idea of how I live to first give a description of my tent. It is a wedge shaped affair, the ridge pole being 6½ feet from the ground which is also about the length and breadth of our floor. At one end of the tent we have cut a hole through the canvas and have had a mud fireplace built. By the side of the fireplace is the door. Across the other side of the tent is a peculiar structure we call our bed. It consists of 4 stakes driven into the ground with poles stretched from a couple of cross pieces, each connecting two of these stakes. On these poles we spread some evergreens and straw and make a comfortable bed. This takes up half our room. In the other half we turn round whenever that difficult operation becomes indispensable.

While we are in camp, all my duty consists in drilling my company for about two hours during the day and—but that is all. Just now however for a day or two I shall be busy making another Muster Roll and that will only give me a temporary employment and then, if the army remains stationary, I shall return to my former idleness. Thus you have a clear idea of my life. The twenty two hours not occupied by drilling is filled up by lounging round into different tents, reading the New York Herald, smoking, and sleeping.

I study tactics but I will get no good from that as I already know the theory pretty well which however is not of the slightest use. I refer to battalion movements, of course. I wouldn't give in to Gen. Scott about company maneuvers. *Voila le tout!*

Tell Em I got a letter from Mattie Steele the other day. I decidedly approve of that young lady. She has common sense without being prosy, wonderful union of good qualities.

I'm well and longing to see you.

Your devoted son,
Stanley

STANLEY'S JOURNAL

January 1, 1863. Near Falmouth, Virginia. A year ago I wrote in this book that I wished the coming year might find me far south. That wish has been fulfilled. I am far south and in as favorable a situation as my fondest hopes could have desired.

By the way I am probably a 1st Lieut. though I have received no official notification of the fact. If Capt. Charlie has resigned as is probable, it is so. . . . Also, I had my pocket picked of every cent I had while in Washington, which was absolutely disgusting. Over $20.00 gone at a flash.

Camp Sykes Division
Near Henry House, Virginia
January 5, 1863

Dear Edwin,

But I am anxious from the way you talk that you should know how I feel about this terrible duty of mine. God knows, I would be inexpressibly glad to know that there would never be need that I should go into battle. I would use every honorable means to keep out of one, and I would resign this moment on that very account did I not sincerely believe and know that ours is the very noblest, holiest cause man ever strove and died for, and because I do believe this from the bottom of [my] heart.

I think that in all this whole army there is not a man who will go into danger more calmly and trustingly than ourself. I say this not boasting but because I can't help believing it and yet I could not die gladly for my country as some have said they could.[6] Life is so dear that I can only be willing to die. I seldom think of such things and only speak now because from some strange misunderstanding it appears that you think I am so babyishly inane as to desire to do that which a true man has to use every strength of body and soul to make himself do.

>Ever yr. Brother and (what's of
>more consequence) yr. friend,
>Stanley

Camp Sykes Division
Near Potomac Creek, Virginia
January 11, 1863

Dear [Sister] Em,

Don't be frightened at the size of my paper.[7] I have no other and you must have this or none. We are doing nothing at all down here on the Rappahannock, nothing at all except trying to keep our noses and our feelings from becoming blue. In the former endeavor, thanks to my Yankee *savoir faire*, I have been quite successful.

I have dug our tent out and made a hole at one end of this extemporized cellar which answers admirably all the purposes of a fireplace. Our chimney consists of two barrels placed over the smoke vent of our subterranean

---

6. Stanley may be referring to his great granduncle, Nathan Hale.
7. The paper is eight inches by twelve inches. Stanley had previously written on paper that is five inches by eight inches.

oven.[8] All together this contrivance, albeit it is painfully suggestive of "our final resting place," nevertheless makes our tent palatial in comparison with those which surround it, and I take no small pride in bragging about it to old fellows who went through the Peninsula campaign and who have hitherto patronized the "new recruit" most provokingly. *Nous averis changes tout cel.* I am now addressed with respect and persons point to me as I walk through the camp and whisper "He has invented the new fireplace"! Officers come and look at the novel affair with admiration while I affably explain the philosophy of it to them. There is no knowing where this thing may stop. At present we bid fair to become a regt. of Troglodytes. Everybody is on fire to emulate our comfort.

Love to all, Stanley

Near Henry House, Virginia
January 11, 1863

Dear Willie,

I have some time and nothing to do so I believe I will write a big note to my little brother. I live in a hole in the ground now and sleep on some poles covered with evergreens. Perhaps you don't think it is nice to do this but it is. I have quite a nice time, living in my cave like Robinson Crusoe.

Twice a day a sergeant comes to me and says "Sir, the patrol is ready." And then I put on my sword and get out of my canvas-covered cave and, sure enough, I see 10 men standing in two rows and they all have guns in their hands. Then I say "Right Face Forward, Route Step MARCH!" and then I draw my sword and march at the head of the party. In this way, I go all round the camp of Gen. Sykes Division, about 3 miles, and when I see any soldier, I look

---

8. Digging out the tent and the chimney were apparently improvements on the "mud fireplace" mentioned above in the letter to Mother from Stanley dated December 29, 1862 on page 176.

very fierce and say "What are you doing here?" And if he cannot give me a pass or some good reason for not being in his camp, I make him march along with my men and as soon as I get back to where I live, I put him in a sort of prison we have for naughty men.

I go out with this "Provost Guard," as these 10 men are called, twice every day and that is all I have to do. Whenever a soldier sees me coming down the road he runs away if he can or hides behind some trees—but I usually catch all such men and it will be exceedingly difficult for you to imagine how remarkably ferocious I am to them when I have caught them. I frown and look as cross as if they had run a pin into me or had pulled my whiskers, which it is now just possible to do, my dear brother. They are then terrified and beg me to let them go, but I say nothing and walk on looking very strait before me, in consequence of which I sometimes stub my toe.

Your loving brother,
Stanley

Stanley's correspondence and journals contained no reference to African-Americans other than the picture enclosed with the January 11, 1863 letter to Willie. John does not appear to be a soldier in uniform, but was probably a southern slave who had escaped—a "contraband." Confederate-owned slaves who sought refuge in Union military camps or who lived in territories that fell under Union control were declared contraband of war[9]: "Regiments needed labor: extra hands to cook meals, wash clothes and dig latrines. When African-American men and women were willing to do these things, whites were happy not to ask inconvenient questions—not the first or last time that the allure of cheap labor would trump political principles in America."[10]

---

9. http://en.wikipedia.org/wiki/Contraband. Last updated October 20, 2011.

10. Adam Goodheart, "The Shrug That Made History," *New York Times Magazine*, April 3, 2011, 59.

This, my brother William Fitz Hale,
is my man John, who both cooks
and brings to me my breakfast,
dinner & supper. This picture is
yours, now be a good boy and deserve
so precious a gift.
                Good bye
                    Stanley

[n.d.]

Dear Stanley,

I am learning to write. This is the first time I ever have written in ink. I thank you very much for your letters and your man John but I think if you live in Robinson Crusoe's hut you had better call your man Friday instead of John.

Willie

———

Near Henry House, Virginia
January 25, 1863

Dear Willie,

There is a small horse here who has a large tail and a very large horse who has an exceedingly small tail. This is very queer indeed. But the reason of it is five times as funny; a sheep ate the big horse's tail all up so that now the poor and bereaved quadruped has hardly so much as a stump left.

It is nice here. I drive horses every day which is good fun. There is a snow fort outdoors and there is going to be a snow man whom I wish you to name. Now you must print me a long letter and tell me what the name shall be and how the forts do at Beverly.

I love you a great deal more than a bushel basket full.

Your brother,
Stanley

———

Near Henry House, Virginia
January 29, 1863

Dear Mattie,

You cannot imagine what a perfect fever of delight I was thrown into by receiving yr. letter tonight. . . . I needed cheering sadly and your letter, so undeservedly friendly, acted as a glass of champagne to a fainting person. . . .

WILLIAM FITZHALE ABBOT
1853–1922

I have something to tell you about at last. The "intermediate" man stands in the way no longer. The Hooker has at last fished the prize he has so long angled for and I was in at the death.[11] It came about in this way. Burnside was reprieved, not pardoned, from Fredericksburg and to save his head he needed success. Wherefore, one cold morning orders came to us, saying "Pack up your duds and move"! The duds were packed and we waited the signal to blast. Everyone said "We are to fight once more." And I was believing what they said.

Now, as perhaps you may remember, I am upon Provost Guard which duty would keep me out of all manner of fighting whatsoever. Indeed, my entire employment would have been to sit on a stump and to reproach all stragglers for being no nearer danger than myself. That would have been fine, would it not? So I asked Maj. Andrews to be temporarily transferred to one of the line companies. After infinite bother the Major, like the unjust judge, did injustice because I "troubled" him and, on the clear, frosty morning of the 20th, I marched out of camp as 1st Lieutenant of "H" Co.

A short march through the frozen fields and we halted before a wood of no inconsiderable dimensions when one remembers how much fuel it takes to keep an army like ours from freezing and also the fact that we were only here miles or so from three or four large encampments—Virginia is fast clearing of trees, I assure you. After a short halt the assembly sounded and we fell in expecting, of course, to continue the march.

But no, on we pushed, a whole division, strait into the woods and halted again. Then we knew we were to bivouac there that night. A half a dozen of the officers, among them myself, had a fire built under a great fir, spread our blankets on the ground, and smoked and talked

---

11. Major General Joseph Hooker was promoted on January 26, 1863 to command the Army of the Potomac, thus supplanting Major General Ambrose Burnside.

the afternoon away. "Why, it is a picnic," said I. Just then
the tip of my nose (had it been Proboscis it would have
been the bridge I suppose) became of a sudden wet. I
looked up to ascertain the cause and another great drop
of rain pelted into my eye. And then it was a picnic only
in a woefully Pickwickian point of view. . . . What a pretty
word "bivouac" is? Yes, but "Beelzebub" too has a pleasing
sonorous sound!

At day break, the ranks were formed once more and
we pushed on, waded on I should say, for the mud was
fathomless. Night found us only six miles from our starting
place, utterly exhausted at that. All day it had poured
and no New England mind can appreciate the success
of Mother Earth's and Daddy Cloud's endeavor to turn
Virginia into a quagmire.

To say I never saw such mud is nothing. I never even
dreamt of one iota of it. Everything was at a deadlock. The
movement was necessarily abandoned and it took two
days spent in corduroying causeways to bring the army
back to its first position, and so my letter is dated still
"Near Henry House."

Well, I can afford to jest about the matter, but with
little relish when I remember the leader, so simple, so
manly and strait forward to whom this affair was death.
Poor Burnside, he really deserved a better fate. And yet
one cannot help laughing to think that he, who fought
Roanoke, Newhorne, Fredericksburg, perished literally
because he got "stuck in the mud"!

This poor man is truly unfortunate. The army hated
him because he succeeded McClellan and attained no
other success. The country hated him because he could
not create pontoons and it seemed he hated himself
because nature had not made him a genius. Is it not pitiful
to see a worthy, honest, mediocre man crushed beneath
the burden of an Atlas?[12] It is nearly the saddest sight in

---

12. Once again, Stanley recognizes a man to be worthy and honest even
     though his actions were ineffective.

the world. I think what a future must there be for Burnside! Think of his self upbraidings!

And "the army of defeat," it has vindicated its name. It claims the soubriquet as a right now. Oh it is not a pleasant thing to be one in an army that has failed. It is right hard to be cheerful sometimes. Success is so bitterly needful and we cannot even strive after success. These bleak cheerless holes covered with mud and stumps and dirty snow are no more dismal than our prospects. But it is wrong to despair. We must make heart and tongue both say that God's way is the best way. Our cause has many a weak and mean and false defender but it has also an infinite Defender and so I think it is best to let the future alone [judge] for after all it is nearly blasphemous to doubt.

It is a good thing to have an enthusiasm. . . . It enables one to say "I believe the sun will shine upon our victory yet."

> So, very truly yr. friend,
> Stanley

⸺∞⸺

> Near Henry House, Virginia
> February 8, 1863

Dear Mother,

But what was it—little Em said? Oh, "she supposed Hooker's men were all very enthusiastic at the promotion of their general." Really I have seen but very little enthusiasm since I left the stay-at-homes. The army is filled with very sober, selfish complaining men just now who still have a remembrance of an old fogy by the name of McClellan and they obstinately persist in saying that it don't make much difference who leads them as long as he is kept from them.

These are fools, are they not? But dear me, when there is so much folly in the world, I am half of the opinion it is wise to humor the folly but the other half of me is however fully convinced that the President is a very wise, firm and sagacious statesman and that his advisers are all "honorable" gentlemen of the most profound judgment and stainless integrity. So every act of theirs must partake of their wisdom, firmness, sagacity, judgment and integrity.

Love to Father and Willie.

Yr. loving son,
Stanley

Camp Sykes Division
Near Henry House, Virginia
February 13, 1863

Dear Mattie,

Do you know that I am really very popular with my men, and it's all owing to a certain talk we once had together. You ended off, you know, by saying that perhaps after all I was right about discipline and all that, but after a little thought I found out that I had been a snob in saying what I did—and yesterday when I was sick and asked one of my men to get me a little wood, I heard him tell a man outside my tent, that he would go a mile on his knees to get it, if none could be got any other way.

I tell you I have given up the machine theory thanks to you. Receiving a kindness is like being tagged, one has to tag somebody else right off and getting a letter makes me feel like tagging all creation. Isn't this a nice little letter from my brother Willie that I enclose to you? You must send it back. I am his favorite brother you must know and the military gentlemen he speaks of are paper soldiers I made for him when I was at home. "Your man John" is a picture I made of my donkey and sent to Willie.

Stanley

Near Falmouth, Virginia
March 1, 1863

Dear Mother,

The company has been relieved of Provost Guard duty much to my delight and now I have to perform the proper duties of a line officer. Last week for the first time I was out on Picket and singularly enough my first experience in that much dreaded duty was quite full of interest.

The rebel cavalry drove in our outer [line] and the Picket reserve (to which I was attached) were ordered under arms to be ready to move at a moment's notice. Taken all in all 'twas quite an affair. We lost two hundred cavalry taken prisoner but the victors wisely refrained from making an attack on our infantry which, in the hilly country, must have resulted in a defeat to them. . . .

I was ordered on a fatigue party, working on entrenchments being thrown up for the protection of "High Bridge" on the railroad half way between Regina Creek and Falmouth. After that I was on as Officer of the Day—so you see that after all there is some duty to be done in the inactive Army of the Potomac.

Your loving son,
Stanley

———◦◦◦———

Camp Sykes Division
March 6, 1863

Dear Cousin Mattie,

I got your delightful letter the other day just when I was so sick and blue that I needed a glass of champagne and your draft did me worlds of good. . . .

I am about to clap my wings and crow. Do you happen to remember a prophecy I made to you one evening that before the year was through our government would be a dictatorship? In sober truth without exaggeration it is really so at the present time. . . . I think Lincoln more absolutely than any monarch on earth possesses the powers of a despot, viz., the supreme control of the army and navy and of the finances together with the might of arbitrary arrest.

Very sincerely, your friend,
Stanley

———

Camp Sykes Division
March 27, 1863

Dear Edwin,

You can hardly imagine how hopeful and happy I feel about the coming movements. Hooker, whatever he may be as a man, is really a far better leader than poor Burnside and there is some foundation of truth in all these puffs he gets in the newspaper about "increasing the efficiency of the army."

I begin to share in the confidence that is growing strong in the army. After all, may not this last ground effort be destined to succeed? Failure now must be final overthrow and I cannot bring myself to believe that our folly and selfishness will be permitted utterly to wreck our cause which is so noble. The army mourns still for its exiled leader, but yet it loves country better even than McClellan, and it will be true and steadfast in the campaign that is upon us. Let us hope that justice will be accomplished yet.

Lovingly, Stanley

———

Camp Sykes Division
March 28, 1863

Dear Cousin Mattie,

Ah, the balmy days of the old republic. The boyhood of our people has gone to come no more. I fear your wish to see once more the "Union as it was" is destined to a disappointment. Many of us seem to forget that this revolution is working in our midst a change as vital as that effected in France at the end of the last century. Whatever that change may be, we can be very sure it can never be a "change back again to what we were" as you hope.

I, for one, believe that we shall be better, purer, more worthy. The noble future God has made possible for us and that is one great reason I hope we shall be wise enough to abandon a system of government which has been proved to be most costly and most inefficient. Let us see what our condition will be in the event of a successful termination of the war (If we are unsuccessful, military despotism is a certainty). We shall find ourselves a nation of soldiers and in a position where a strong government will be a *sine qua non*, for some years at least, in order to keep down the alienated South.

Can elections be permitted to go on uncontrolled? . . . Our government must, I fear, continue to be in some measure elective but it cannot be to anything like the extent it has been in time past for at the outset the reestablishment of the national integrity implies the enslavement of half the nation. Mind I never saw that we would be so lucky as to get an hereditary monarchy these fifty years. What I do say however is that the power will necessarily be erroneously centralized. At least, that is the price we will have to pay for union if we buy it. Well you are saying, and very properly too, that all this is guesswork, so perhaps we had better agree to disagree.

Have you curiosity to know the future I had chalked out for myself? It was this, very humble, with the clink of no money in it. One day before I went to Exeter to prepare for college I went down to the sea shore to an old revolutionary redoubt from whence in times gone by 3 guns had frowned upon the pretty bay at the head of which nestled the sleepy town of Beverly.[13] I curled myself

---

13. This is most likely a reference to the site of what is today Beverly's Independence Park. In response to the mayor's request for historical facts when the park's name was changed from Queen's Park to Independence Park in 1906, Charles Woodbury wrote: "On the eastern side or parade ground was a battery of three guns. . . . These guns were mounted on carriages, and were ordered by General Washington to be sent from Framingham for the defense of the town." Charles Woodbury, "Independence Park, Beverly, Massachusetts." Joint Standing Committee on Printing, Beverly, Massachusetts, 1906, 1–2.

up under the grassy rampart and looked out on the water
on which the dazzling sunlight lay fashioning in my mind
the life I would live. I would go to college and learn how
to think and write. I would get some teacher's place in a
country academy and make the distasteful drudgery of
6 hours earn the bread for 24 and bye and bye, when I
was thirty years old and more, I would begin in leisure
moments to write things that somehow I felt would be in
my heart to say.

As I settled upon this future I gave a great sigh because
it was not very brilliant, and that was the first and last time
I was ever displeased with the prospect. The determination
to carry it out remained quite firm until this war came
upon us and so I came into the army and so God has
made my future easier and happier than I intended. If my
life is spared me, what better position can be imagined for
a person who wished to write, but who cannot bear the
thought of trying to make a livelihood out of the fancies
that he loves, than the position I shall occupy? And if my
life is not spared me what more beautiful death is possible?
Indeed I believe with you in special providences, and
because I believe in them, I think it is very safe to leave
our destiny without a doubt or a murmur in the hollow of
His hand.

Sincerely,
your friend Stanley

CHAPTER 12

---❀---

BATTLE OF CHANCELLORSVILLE
MARCH, 1863–MAY, 1863

> Army of the Potomac, army of brave men,
> Beaten again and again but never quite broken,
> You are to have the victory in the end
> But these bleak months are your anguish.
> —STEPHEN VINCENT BENÉT, *John Brown's Body*

The long winter bivouac of inactivity was about to end. Except for the disastrous "mud march," Stanley, along with the rest of the Army of the Potomac, had nothing to do but stay warm, post pickets to monitor the activities of the Confederates, and prepare for future battles. With the arrival of spring, the Army was ready to move into action once more.

STANLEY'S JOURNAL

March 27, 1863. Two months and ten days with no record and, now that they are passed, I can recall no event worthy of being recorded. Our fizzle on the 20th of Jan. succeeding my last entry has become history. All the rest of the time I have been eating and sleeping and trying to keep warm. Capt. Goddard has got out into the field at last.[1] Of

---

1. Captain Charles Goddard, commander of Stanley's Company A, was a friend of Edwin's. He had been stationed at Ft. Preble to recruit and train new soldiers.

course we are no longer Provost Guard. . . . We are going to move in good earnest in a short time now and then perhaps I may have something to say.

When I was out on picket last I lay on my back, kicked up my heels, and composed the following which behold in memoriam.

There is a shady nook
Amongst the murmuring pines,
Close by a prattling brook
Arch'd o'er by clustering vines.

It is a soldier's bower,
Where his weary limbs are laid
When his lonely watch is o'er
And his picket round is made.

There come to him fair visions
Of love and friends and home,
Vain slumberous illusions
Whose substance ne'er shall come.

Sometimes his dreams will picture
Sweet scenes of long ago.
The days of love's young rapture
His mother's whisper low.

Sometimes attained ambitions
Paint gladness on his face,
More dear than the traditions
That to his past gave grace.

But ever are his dreamings
Fairer than ought that's true,
Fairer than his rememberings,
Aye, and his hopings too.

And when the morn hath come
And Phoebus' leveled spears,
He wakes and leaves a home
Where he hath shed no tears.

Wherefore he comes in after days
To think of that green bower
Where Fanny sang to him sweet lays
Thro' many a careless hour.

STANLEY'S JOURNAL[2]

April 11, 1863. Still the Army lingers and still the papers declare that it is absolutely going to move next week at farthest, probably tomorrow. Meantime, I study tactics, read Lever, watch for letters, and kill more time than secessionists. Altogether I am in good spirits. The campaign must soon open and the time approaches when I shall be able to know of what stuff I am made.

At present I am in a curious state of doubt whether I am a hero or a coward.

Camp Sykes Division
April 13, 1863

Dear Cousin Mattie,

Papa Abraham has been down to see us lately and was finally received by his children.[3] We've had any quantity of reviews and inspections and everything goes to show that Mrs. Hooker is going to break up housekeeping at no distant date—report says she is going to move to Richmond. Hope she'll have a pleasant journey, I'm sure.

As for me, I have got entirely well now and am in fine spirits and health, all ready for the campaign. . . . I do love priding and display . . . and that's one reason I am glad that I'm a soldier. The blue and gold and black feathers and crimson sash have an immense attraction for me and it's delightful to walk majestically about camp with a jangling sword by my side. I can't help thinking sometimes how absurd it is, for me at least, to twaddle about "sacrifice" and all that in entering the service.

You can hardly imagine how grand and heroic I felt as I stalked up to the Adjutant's table at Fort Preble and wrote "Edward S. Abbot, Student" on the enlistment papers. I actually made my will beforehand. . . . Do you know I sometimes feel almost [guilty] that my "patriotism" has

2. This is the last entry in Stanley's journal.
3. Pesident Lincoln.

been so profitable? It is hateful to make money by serving a cause for which one had made up one's mind to die!

Sincerely,
your friend Stanley

———

Near Henry House, Virginia
April 17, 1863

Dear Mother,

You must not think my thoughts of you are few because my letters have grown infrequent. Not an hour passes without its loving remembrance of my Mother but of late I have been very, very busy and when leisure comes I have no heart for writing. . . .

In the future I fear I will be obliged to keep a still more perfect silence for everything betokens a speedy commencement of active operations and once in motion opportunities of writing will be few and far between . . . so you must expect few letters and short ones.

All this reminds me of something you say about "dreading to hear of some terrible advance" and the anxiety it will cause you. Dear, dear Mother, what can I say to you? How can I let you know the eagerness with which I look forward to the "terrible advance"? I appreciate perfectly well how much more difficult it is to be brave for others than it is to be brave for ourselves but still is it not equally a duty?

You know I would not have you love me less but it makes the tears come to my eyes to think that, even involuntarily, I cause you additional pain and anxiety. I would give anything to know that you were at peace about me. You must not think of the "hardships" that some wretched egotists in the army delight to brag about and to exaggerate fearfully. Be it understood. All that will be mere pleasure to me. I actually love this hand to mouth style of living. It has all the charms of a picnic for me.

Yr. loving son,
Stanley

Stanley's unit traveled from Falmouth to Yorktown about April 15. The reason for the trip is not known. However, Stanley does comment in his April 13 letter to Mattie, "Everything goes to show that Mrs. Hooker is going to break up housekeeping at no distant date—report says she is going to move to Richmond." Perhaps he went to Yorktown in connection with the possibility of an attack from that location on Richmond. In any event, Stanley quickly returned to Henry House so as to participate in the Battle of Chancellorsville starting on May 1. He was promoted to First Lieutenant on April 27, 1863, just before the battle.

April 20, 1863

Dear [Sister] Emmie,

Here I am at last quietly in camp within six miles of Yorktown. We sailed on Tuesday.[4]. . . We carried most of our horses (mine among the number) on our boat, the Commodore. Wed. we started and arrived at Fortress Monroe about 5 P.M., landed our horses, and spent the night on board the boat. Next day arrived the most awful confusion you ever saw. We got our things ashore all mixed up and had them carried to a camp some four miles off near Hampton.

The Monitor was in full view (not from bed) and is excellently described by Secessionists, as "a cheese on a raft." Next day, Friday, we moved on to Big Bethel and camped on the battleground of last spring waiting all day for our wagons and only getting them after dark. Next day, Saturday, we moved to our present position within six miles of Yorktown. Gen. B.[5] and I went forward and made a sort of reconnaissance to within about 1½ miles of the town, where our advance now is. We could see their works very plainly, and count their guns etc. etc. A long time (an

---

4. April 20, 1863 was a Monday. He sailed on the preceding Tuesday, which was April 14, 1863.
5. The identity of "Gen. B." is unknown.

IRON-CLAD *MONITOR*

hour) we were in a deserted house watching them ride and walk round with our glasses.

Goodnight.

Stanley

The 17th Regiment was at the front of the Sykes Division troops that encountered the Confederates about 11:00 A.M. on May 1 to start the Battle of Chancellorsville.[6] Markers at the site of "Day One of the Chancellorsville Battlefield" state: "One Union officer recalled that his men advanced 'steadily and with a will, although exposed to a sharp fire from musketry and artillery. . . .' Confederate forces under General Lafayette McLaws poured a devastating fire into the Union troops. . . .

"McLaws' job was to hold the Federals in his front while his commander Gen. Thomas J. 'Stonewall' Jackson 'would

6. See maps of the positions of Federal and Confederate units at the National Park Service Chancellorsville Battle Center, Fredericksburg, Virginia, as well as on their website: http://www.nps.gov/frsp/history culture/trpmaps.htm

endeavor to gain the rear of the enemy.' Jackson did just that."
This enabled the Confederates to attack the Union flank on
the next two days. Stanley described the impact of this initial
encounter on his regiment at the beginning of his May 7 letter
to Edwin below.

Following its heavy losses, Stanley's 17th Regiment was
withdrawn to a position near the route to the United States
Ford and away from the action. They did not confront the
Confederates again during this battle, but were in a position
to cover the retreat across the United States Ford to the Falmouth side of the Rappahannock River. Stanley's map repre-
sents his perspective and does not totally agree with the maps
at the Chancellorsville Battle Center.

> Camp near Henry House
> May 7, 1863

Dear Edwin,

Our reg't was the very first engaged [in the Battle of
Chancellorsville] and lost heavily, more heavily than in
any action at which it has been present. Three officers were
hit, one of them killed dead on the spot. That was on the
first instant.

The army was not beaten whatever the papers may
say. On the 2nd our right was drawn back, and our left
also gave ground next day—but our last position was held,
and could have been held in defiance of any effort of the
enemy. Events unknown to us have compelled the retreat
which was perfectly successful and unmolested except at
the very last. Our Division covered the recrossing of the
Rappahannock and suffered slightly from the enemy's
batteries. The battle was fought near Chancellorsville
about six miles from Fredericksburg and all I know about it
is as follows.

On the 28th, 3 corps crossed at Kelly's Ford—30 miles
upriver and moved down across the Rapidan towards
United States Ford, 8 miles from Falmouth. At this last
point 3 more corps crossed before the 1st moved forward
from the river forming a line of battle extending from a run

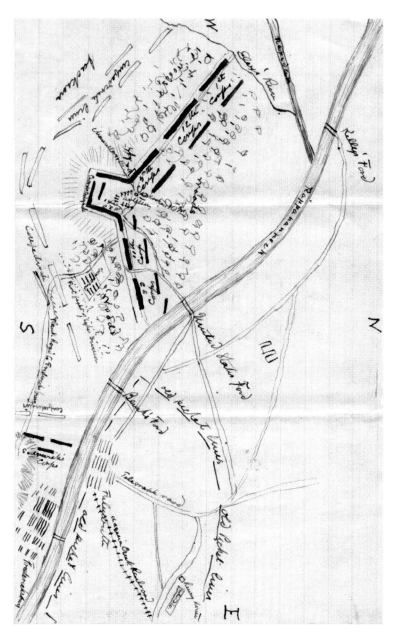

STANLEY'S MAP OF THE BATTLE OF CHANCELLORSVILLE[7]

7. Enclosed with letter to Edwin dated May 7, 1863.

shortly distant from the Rapidan to a point near United States Ford.

Sykes Division was near the centre. A reconnaissance made on the 1st by that Division revealed the fact of the presence of Lee in heavy force. That evening the 11th corps on our right was beaten in and next morning our left also retired before an overwhelming attack which was however finally and completely repulsed.

On the three succeeding days the enemy by desperate fighting failed in gaining an inch. Our final line formed an angle slightly obtuse near the vertex of which we were posted. On the night of the 6th we fell back, and the whole army recrossed the river, as I said, at U.S. Ford.

Meantime, Sedgwick's corps had taken the height of Fredericksburg and pushed up towards our position. It was, however, driven back and forced to recross at Banks Ford close to Falmouth. Our loss is estimated at from 8 to 10 thousand. The enemy's must have been far greater for our positions were very strong. . . .

The musketry fire was heavier, so old officers say, than even at Antietam or Gaines Mills. Undoubtedly the affair is disastrous—but not hopelessly so—Oh for McClellan. The cause of our failure I take to be that in dividing our forces we made it necessary to assume the offensive. We did not do so. Consequently Lee was enabled to crush Sedgwick while amusing Hooker.—It is neither wise nor right to say more. I firmly believe that Hooker will yet beat them if he is not removed. God will protect the right.

For myself, I am well and satisfied that I shall be made strong enough to do my duty faithfully. I find it very hard to be brave without allowing evil thoughts of hatred and anger to master me—but, I know that it is wrong, and will be stronger next time. It drives the devil into my heart to hear those screaming demons rush at us through the smoke!

Make Mother believe that if it is my duty to remember God's presence in the battlefield, she too must trust that. He is there to guard me from all that can really harm.

Lovingly,
Stanley

CHAPTER 13

A BRAVE AND NOBLE MAN
MAY, 1863–JULY, 1863

All goes onward and outward, nothing collapses,
And to die is different from what any one supposed,
    and luckier.
                    —WALT WHITMAN, *Song of Myself*

Stanley was pleased with his life as an officer in the Regular Army. He remained optimistic about the outcome of the war to preserve the Union in spite of the recent defeat at the Battle of Chancellorsville.

                    Camp Sykes Division
                    May 5, 1863

Dear Cousin Mattie,

The bitter fact is we have met with a grave disaster [at Chancellorsville] which will undoubtedly compel the inactivity of this army for months to come. . . . At any rate we will whip them at last. Forty years the Hebrews wandered in search of the Promised Land but at last they reached it. We too shall surely see the fulfillment of the heavenly promise. The God of justice in Heaven shall yet smile on them that fight for justice upon earth. I see a future for my country more noble than has been permitted to any land thus far, a people just, tolerant, peaceful, giving freedom and education to a continent and true to the principles for which they have suffered.

Stanley

~∞∞~

Beverly, Massachusetts
May 17, 1863

My very dear son,

I can never describe to you the immense relief it gave me last Monday morning to have Edwin put your letter into my hands as I called for a moment at his office. I had thought on Saturday and Sunday that I had reasonable assurance of your deliverance from danger in the late contests because your name was not on any discoverable list of killed or wounded . . . but to see it in your own blessed handwriting. Oh Stanley, you would need to be a mother to thoroughly understand the lightening of the load which had oppressed me for several days!

Most heartily do I thank God who preserved you in your hours of peril—but more grateful still am I towards Him for the comfort derived from the tone of feeling expressed in your letter.

Every communication received from you, my precious child, makes me feel more and more convinced that it was, with your convictions, your duty to arm yourself in your country's cause and also that it became my duty to lay aside my womanly fears and give you up to all the risks you must encounter in so doing. God alone knows the struggle it cost me!

You have now had your first experience of the horrors of a battlefield, and not only do I perceive that your courage blanched not, but what gives me far more courage for you, that you strove to fight as a Christian soldier should. Fear not that while she has the assurance that you are striving to conquer the foes within as well as without, your mother will also be striving for that "trust in Him who can alone keep you from all that can really harm you."

I am sure that, since you desire it, strength will be given you "to be brave without having wicked thoughts of hatred and revenge master you." I am also sure that, if I rightfully desire it, He will either preserve my beloved from danger or bind up my broken heart if evil befall him. So let us trust always in Him.

Write when you can to your ever loving Mother.

———

Camp near Henry House,
Virginia
May 18, 1863

Dear Edwin,

You ask me if I like my new life. To tell the truth I have hardly ever thought whether I did or not. I came down here quite convinced that it was the correct thing to do under the circumstances and I have not bothered my head much about the question of liking or disliking. Upon consideration, however, I am inclined to think that I do like it. . . . At any rate my late experiences have convinced me that I can make a good officer and when one feels that he means and is able to do his duty, I question if it's in the power of ordinary circumstances to make him unhappy.

With oceans of love,
Stanley

———

On picket above
Falmouth, Virginia
May 24, 1863

Dear Mattie,

On a Virginian hillside are four stakes, the tops of which are useful since they support a shelter tent, "anglice," a piece of cotton cloth six feet by twelve, and thereby make a shade most grateful in this weary, sun scorched land. Around me, over me, under me, on all sides of me creep, fly, crawl, bite, buzz, and sting myriads of bugs, spiders, mosquitoes, wasps, bees, hornets, road ticks, snails, lizards, flies of every known, and numberless unknown species, blue bottle, triangular, green, yellow, gray, black, and scarlet in five millions of every disgusting bug, insect, or animalculae which nature has cursed mankind of producing.

In this Pandemonium I suffer and I write where are gathered together all animate objects gifted with the power of excoriating humanity. Myself and my countless companions have just finished dinner, that is, I have been eating ham and eggs and bugs (chiefly bugs) while they have been masticating ham, eggs, and officer so its nearly an even thing between us or would be if they would only play fair and leave off when I do which I'm sorry to say they don't seem inclined to do.

Bad luck to 'em. But as I say—dinner is over and the blazing sun is keeping me under a hotter and more galling force than I faced at Chancellorsville. Nothing on earth to do except to hopelessly computate the number of days it will take the concentrated horrors of this frightful country to drive me to madness. So in utter despair I take my pen and paper from my haversack determined to fulminate one last anathema against the demons of earth and air who are about to compass my destruction.

Alas, I feel that I can meet the rebels with a firm heart and hand but spiders. Ugh! No, I must succumb ere long and I beg of you shed a tear of compassion when you read my epitaph which is truthful, "He died of bugs and animalculae." By the way, in my list of enemies I neglected to mention ants, just as the old lady hunted for her spectacles when they were on her nose—nose did I say? Yes, I've killed twenty ants who have even penetrated to that citadel of dignity—the proboscis.

Sincerely yr. friend Stanley

On picket above
Falmouth, Virginia
May 25, 1863

Dear Mother,

As for the future, inactivity seems to be our destiny for perhaps months to come, which however distasteful it may be to me, probably is pleasing to my own dear anxious Mother. . . .

I am well and perfectly contented except that it's rather hard to read the accounts of our successes in the west and feel no impatience at that evil destiny which has made the history of this army a dreary monotony of idleness or defeat, but I have not even yet ceased to hope that the time will come when fortune will cease to persecute us. I have faith to believe we will enter Richmond after all.

Ever so much love to Father, Em and Willie. I am perfectly delighted that you are going to Meadville.[1] It is just what you need and it will take off my mind the heaviest load I have to bear to know that you are gaining strength and enjoying yourself with Frank and Katie.

Yr. own loving son,
Stanley

Near Henry House, Virginia
June 1, 1863

Dear Mattie,

You ask me "what were my feelings before, in and after the battle [at Chancellorsville]"?—Very unromantic I assure you. When we were marching into the open space on May Day, my chief attention was devoted to a "hard tack" for biscuit, which constituted my breakfast. While we were making our famous charge across the fields, I was so busy keeping the men in line that I'm inclined to think

1. Stanley's mother was planning a visit to Frank, who was studying at the seminary in Meadville, Pennsylvania at this time.

I did not have much time for a metaphysical examination into the state of my moral and intellectual condition and, after the affair was over, my first thought was to get hold of a canteen and my next—Well there was no next for I tumbled down under a tree and went to sleep.

I had a delicious dream. It was of lemonade and oyster pie. I was waked up by a tremendous fury on our left and, two minutes after, the rebels attacked our lines. We soon though sent them back the way they came or at least sent some of them back and a good share of them on a longer journey yet. I must confess that a battle is not impressive [in] which one is engaged himself although to a spectator it is the grandest thing in the world.

> Very sincerely,
> yr. friend Stanley

Sykes Division awakened on June 4 to a 1:00 A.M. reveille call at Falmouth with orders to break camp at 3:00 A.M. It proceeded upriver to defend against an anticipated crossing of the Rappahannock River at one of the fords near Lee's army. Instead, Lee's army was traveling north in the Shenandoah Valley on the other side of the mountains with the intention of bringing the war to the northern states.

> Near Henry House, Virginia
> June 11, 1863

Dear [Sister] Emmie,

At 1 A.M. Thurs. June 4th the sleeping camp was roused by an order from Brig. Hdqtrs. To be ready to start at 3 A.M that same night—the thing was all utter surprise to everyone. However, we leaped out of our comfortable beds, struck tents, packed our valises and blankets, drew rations and in two hours were ready to start. And so in the still darkness we moved away from the place which for 9 months has been a home to our Division. For the fourth time we leave and I think this time forever. Eleven o'clock next day found us 8 miles upriver—2 miles above

Banks Ford to the beautiful open country.[2] The road leads through shady woods, across cozy New England like farms, pretty streams and rolling hills, and it was a great delight to escape from the barren desolated oasis of sterility the army has created in the heart of this beautiful country.

So goodbye. Lovingly,
Stanley

In the midst of picket duty to monitor the enemy across the Rappahannock River, Stanley experienced a peaceful encounter with a southern soldier, who may have put him in mind of his Harvard friend, MacElrath.

Camp Sykes Division
June 11, 1863

Dear Mattie,

Meantime we linger on not unpleasantly on the brink of this river so peaceful in appearance that one forgets the sword he wears in looking at it. When I was on picket the other day, I swam across to the southern side and had a long chat with a confederate officer. We got along admirably and he gave me the paper which I brought over between my teeth and which I sent to you knowing your fondness for curiosities. The officer (he belonged to the 4th Cavalry) said that on the 1st of May we were opposed to Anderson's whole corps! 15 thousand strong, and that he knew we were regulars because we deployed by regt. and double quicked straight at them, giving them no time to [aim] their artillery with effect. The volunteers, he said, "creep up. You ran."

Our Division, the only one engaged, numbered less than 5,000 and we drove them a mile and would be driving

2. "Burbank's brigade settled down with Sykes Headquarters staff at Benson's Mills within easy reach of any of three crossings" of the Rappahannock River: Banks Ford, United States Ford, Richard's Ford. Timothy Reese, *Sykes' Regular Infantry Division, 1861–1864: A History of Regular United States Infantry Operations in the Civil War's Eastern Theater* (Jefferson, North Carolina: McFarland & Company, 1990), 229.

them still had not Hooker's order forced us to retreat. It is not unpleasant to find one's enemies in such a state of mind in regard to the regulars. But I won't brag any more.

What a queer paper is that I sent you, old in appearance as some revolutionary sheet. But for all that, the editorial is very able, though sophistical. It is liberal, clever, and effective. Do you notice the pleasing moderation and freedom from brag and vaporing throughout the whole paper? Compare that with our more pretentious ones and I hardly think we gain by the comparison.

I can't help admiring these people. Their devotion and earnestness are real and they fight admirably. They fight for the world's retrogression, to perpetuate a faulty past, not to chalk out a better future, and so they must be destroyed without mercy as the enemies of progress. Yet one can pity and even admire them or rather one can't help doing so.

Yours truly,
Stanley

The following two letters were the last ones written by Stanley four days before his fatal wound. Edwin found them with Stanley's effects after he died.

Camp near
Frederick, Maryland
June 28, 1863

Dear Edwin,

We halt today and I take this opportunity of dropping you a line, in the vague hope that I may find some opportunity of sending it. We left Banks Ford on the 13th inst. and since that time have neither received nor sent out a mail.[3] The army is rapidly concentrating in the neighborhood of Frederick [Maryland] and without doubt

---

3. "A mail sack had arrived at Benson's Mills, tossed into a baggage wagon when they pulled back from the river. It had been forgotten in all the bustle." Reese, *Sykes' Regular Infantry Division*, 231.

South Mountain is to be the scene of another bloody engagement. Lee is said to be at that point fortifying.

We will have hot work dislodging him if that is the case, for the position is naturally of immense strength, and it is a standing wonder in the army how Burnside carried it so easily last fall. It was, as far as can be known now, most shameful negligence to permit the rebel army to slip past us, and I am thankful that the President has carried out his usual Carthaginian policy and given us a new commander.[4]

How Meade will do, it would be foolish to predict as he is simply unknown.—He may be "the coming man" for all we know, but why?—Why leave the thing to chance?— Why not give us the chosen leader whose very name would be more to us than 50,000 men? It is a significant fact, as far at least as my observation has gone, that officers and men regard the ultimate return of McClellan as a sure thing, of course. Oh would that it were so!

We have made some terrible marches since we broke camp, especially that from Warrenton Junction to Manassas Junction. On that day 9 men dropped down dead on the road from our Division alone. One volunteer regt. 450 strong came into camp at nightfall with 1 Major, 1 Lieutenant and 5 men!

> With much love to all,
> goodbye—lovingly Stanley

Bivouac near
Frederick, Maryland
June 28, 1863

Dear Mattie,

The first mail we have rec'd since the 13th has . . . come in and brought to me among other letters your most welcome and angelic one, for which many thanks. . . .

---

4. President Lincoln replaced General Hooker with General Meade as commander of the Army of the Potomac on June 28, 1863.

No wonder you were bewildered by the newspapers for I much question if anyone in the country has been more completely non-plussed and astounded than Maj. Gen. Hooker, our . . . commander. As far as can be known now, it was a disgraceful blunder to allow Lee to slip away from us as he has done and, for once, I heartily approve of the Carthaginian policy of the President in removing unsuccessful generals. . . .

The main facts appear to be that Lee amused us at Falmouth while he transferred his command to the Shenandoah Valley, pushed up into Maryland and thence into the Cumberland Valley, Pa. As soon as the fact was known, we broke camp and by forced marches brought the entire army by way of Warrenton Junction, Manassas, and Centreville to the Bull Run or Kettoctan [Catoctin] Range, where we remained four or five days, our lines stretching fr. Thoroughfare Gap to Leesburg and the Potomac. While at Aloha I watched through my glass the cavalry fight at Upperville and Ashby's Gap which was simply an effort of Hooker's to learn the whereabouts of Lee.

Three days after that, on the 26th, that is, we moved forward, crossed the river at Edwards Ferry, and pushed forward to within two miles of the Monacacy which river we forded next day and the same afternoon reached our present camp about 3 miles south of Frederick near which the army appears to be rapidly concentrating. Everything now points to another battle at South Mountain and Antietam. . . .

The recent marches were very severe, especially that fr. Warrenton to Manassas Junction. During that march 9 men fr. our Division alone dropped down dead on the road. The heat was terrible, 90 deg. in the shade and dust. Oh such dust! I myself am well and fresh as need be.

Goodbye,
Stanley

Following days of heavy marches in hot, humid weather, Ayres Division arrived at Gettysburg on the morning of July

2 to rest near the Baltimore Pike behind the defensive "fish-hook" battle line of the Union forces.[5] The division was ready to move as reinforcements or replacements wherever needed. In midafternoon, the order came to proceed closer to the battle—to the intersection of the Taneytown and Wheatfield roads, just behind Little Round Top. At 4:00 P.M. the order was to move forward into action. The official report of Brigade Commander Col. Sidney Burbank reads:

> At this time the brigade occupied on the left side of an extremely rough and rocky hill [Little Round Top], the right extending into the woods and some heavy under-growth. The whole line moved forward to the foot of the hill and out of the woods to the edge of a wide marsh [Plum Run], extending across its whole front, and soon after across this marsh at a double-quick, and ascended to the crest of the hill on the opposite side [Houck's Ridge], and moved forward to some shelter near a woods. . . . I ordered my line forward to a fence and stone wall on the edge of the woods [Rose's Woods]. . . . A heavy fire opened on our right flank. . . . The enemy was seen at this time moving through a wheat-field to our rear and the brigade was withdrawn as rapidly and in as good order as the nature of the ground would permit. In doing so, however, the troops were exposed to a heavy fire on both flanks, and the loss of officers and men was very severe.[6]

When Edwin traveled to Gettysburg to retrieve Stanley's body for reburial at Beverly he learned the details of Stanley's last day. He describes Stanley's wounding, death, and burial in his written memorial.

---

5. General Ayres replaced General Sykes as commander of the Second Division on June 28, 1863.
6. *The War of the Rebellion: A Compilation of the Official Records of the Union and Confederate Armies*, vol. XXVII (Washington, D.C.: Government Printing Office, 1880), 645.

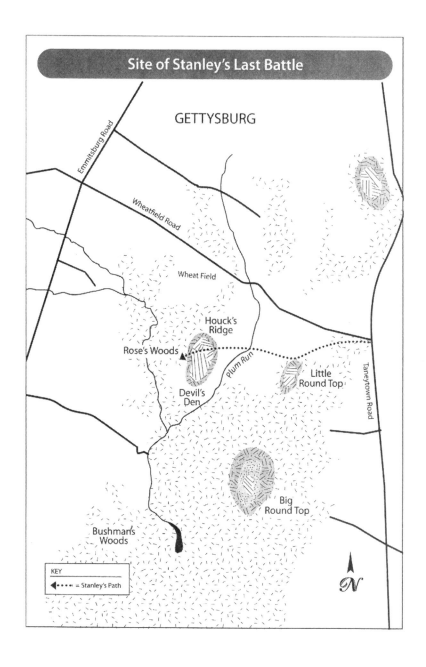

Site of Stanley's Last Battle

GETTYSBURG

Emmitsburg Road

Wheatfield Road

Wheat Field

Houck's Ridge

Rose's Woods

Plum Run

Devil's Den

Little Round Top

Taneytown Road

Big Round Top

Bushman's Woods

KEY

◄••••• = Stanley's Path

N

Early in the fight, while leading his men in a charge down a hill across a marsh and wall and up a little slope, Stanley was struck in the right breast by a minié-ball. The shoulder-strap on the light blouse he wore had worked forward, and the ball, just stripping off some of its gold-lace, passed through the right lung and lodged near the spine. He fell senseless to the ground, and for some hours was unconscious. He was at once borne to the rear, though not expected to survive long. . . .

A brother officer, who lay by his side until he died, told me that Stanley, when he first became conscious, sat up, and spoke in a full, natural tone. He lay in a hospital tent on some straw. The tent was pitched in a grove on a hill, around the foot of which a beautiful brook flowed.

On Tuesday morning, when the surgeon, Dr. Billings, of the Regular service, came in, Stanley asked the Doctor to feel his pulse, and desired to know if he was feverish, since the pulsations were at one time strong and quick and then slow and feeble. Dr. Billings, a most excellent surgeon and a very prompt and straightforward man, felt of the pulse and then, looking Stanley in the eye, slowly answered, "No, Mr. Abbot, there is no fever there. You are bleeding internally. You never will see to-morrow's sunset."

Captain Walcott, the officer at his side, who related these circumstances to me, says that he then looked at Stanley, to see the effect of these words. But Stanley was entirely calm. Presently he said, with a smile, "That is rather hard, isn't it? But it's all right; and I thought as much ever since I was hit. . . ."

My brother's grave was marked carefully with a wooden headboard, made from a box cover, and bearing his name, rank, and day of death. It was so suitable a place for a soldier to sleep, that I was reluctant to remove the body for any purpose. But the spot was part of a private farm; and as removal must come, I thought it best to take the body home, and lay it with the dust of his kindred. When my companions had scraped the little and light earth away, there he was wrapped in his gray blanket, in so natural a posture, as I had seen him lie a hundred times in sleep, that it seemed as if he must awake at a word.

Two soldiers of the Eleventh Infantry, the companion regiment of the Seventeenth, had followed me to the spot,—one a boy hardly as old as Stanley, the other a man of forty. As the body was lifted from the grave, this boy of his own accord sprang forward, and gently taking the head, assisted in laying the body on the ground without disturbing it. . . . I told them to uncover the face. They did so, and I recognized the features, though there was nothing pleasant in the sight. I then bade them replace the folds of the gray blanket, his most appropriate shroud, and lay the body in the coffin. They did so; but again the boy stepped forward, and of his own motion carefully adjusted the folds as they were before.

When we turned to go, I spoke to the boy and his companion. They said they knew Stanley, and knowing I had come for his body, they had left the camp to help me, because they had liked Stanley.

"Yes," added the boy, "he was a strict officer, but the men all liked him. *He was always kind to them.*" That was his funeral sermon. And, by a pleasant coincidence, as one of the men remarked to me on our way back, the sun shone out during the ten minutes we were at the grave, the only time it had appeared for forty-eight hours.[7]

In the letter to Sister Emmie on December 15, 1861, written before he entered the Army, Stanley wrote:

Every man that can strike a blow will be bitterly missed if he dare not come forward in his country's time of agony—I cannot be such a man, Em. I think it is a glorious thing when one has a chance to be a hero.

I used to read, when I was a little boy, of brave and noble men and wish that I might be a brave and noble man myself. . . . The possibility of becoming such is offered

---

7. Abbot, "Edward Stanley Abbot," 426–430.

once to each and all. Woe to him that dare not grasp at the prize when it is within his reach.[8]

Yr. loving brother,
Stanley

Stanley grasped at the prize and attained it. He died a brave and noble man on behalf of the noblest cause of his time—the preservation of the Union.

---

8. To read it in its entirety, see the letter to Emmie from Stanley dated December 15, 1861 on page 97.

CHAPTER 14

CONDOLENCES

For Lycidas is dead, dead ere his prime,
Young Lycidas, and hath not left his peer:
Who would not sing for Lycidas? he knew
Himself to sing, and build the lofty rhyme.
—JOHN MILTON, *Lycidas*

Those who knew and corresponded with Stanley during his life wrote to his parents after his death. They enrich our understanding of Stanley through their own understanding of him.

> Detroit, Michigan
> July 17, 1863
>
> Dear Father and Mother,
>
> I have just received your letters, with Susie's, Emmie's, and the copy of Edwin's. I will not deny it took me a long time to read them through my tears but the first bitterness of the blow is over and, being alone among strangers, with none to weep with me for the brave true heart that has ceased to beat, I come instinctively to you. . . .
>
> Stanley is indeed safe at last, and I think no one of us, in the bitterest pang of sorrow, would wish to call him back. He died so nobly, so bravely, so like a true soldier of Christ, that we would not for the world strip his last moments of their simple beauty. I cannot but think him peculiarly blessed in being privileged to lay down his life in such a cause for it is worth every drop of blood in this

country of ours. I was not worthy to meet such a destiny, or God would have made my duty clear to go; but if He had left us the choice of dying as we would, I would have chosen so to die. And I feel it a duty not to grudge our best and dearest to such a cause, for "the Lord loveth a cheerful giver."

It makes me inexpressibly sad to think that, during these last years in which Stanley had grown into his ripe and generous manhood, I had no opportunity to mark this growth and know him as he developed into the Christian's life. I know that when I left him, we loved each other dearly and enjoyed a peculiar sympathy together; but we corresponded seldom and I looked forward to meeting him with almost a heartsick eagerness to see if we were still all we had been to each other.

And when I heard he was wounded, the sting of sorrow was deadened somewhat by the hope of seeing him more speedily and nursing him in his illness. But now all that hope is swept away and I cannot keep back the tears if I try. Yet I know he grew daily nearer to God and I feel I am growing nearer to Him too; and so I know we must at last find our hearts attuned to a more beautiful harmony than we ever knew before.

Most tenderly,
Frank E. Abbot

Boston
Sunday, July 19, 1863

My dear Mrs. Abbot,

Our conversations during the last two years have been chiefly occasioned by the death of persons dear to us, and for this new bereavement I can find no comfort for either. For a long time past Stanley has never been on any day out of my mind. I have not written to him since we parted, nor was it easy to have found him. I think he did not expect it. Had I known how soon I should lose him I should have done so. . . .

I do not know how I could have averted his fate. I at first strongly dissuaded him from going but soon saw it would be in vain. I asked him if he knew how small was his chance of surviving the war. He said "All of us are but seeking some honourable death," and I would not vex him with opposition. I hoped the best till the very last when now we have no hope any more. Never have I undervalued the risk, never the loss. From human captivity I could have ransomed him, but not from that of Death and I have now no consolation save that I never neglected him while he was with me but made him as happy as I could.

'Tis now nearly thirteen years since I first saw him and loved him at sight. He too loved me. We never ceased to grow nearer each other till, when he went into business and could enjoy nothing, we were for a year at a standstill. But when he began to fit for college we went on again growing together more closely than before. I asked him to take Frank's place during his absence and join me in reading on Saturday nights which pleased him but we could not be much together save in his vacation.

In one of these we were at Stow, and were caught in a thunderstorm in a very dark night while returning from a sail on the river.[1] We could see nothing. I landed from the boat and made a long walk to find the mooring and he was to follow my voice when found. I called again and again but got no answer. 'Twas a dreadful moment. At last I heard his voice, and when we met he told me he had fallen into the water and would not tell me till he was safe, lest it should alarm me. He saw my shock and I his generosity and we felt in one and the same moment our real value to each other. We were scarcely out of each other's arms.

During that week oh little did I think he was saved but for these shambles. Since that night I am certain that we have neither of us liked to go a long time without meeting. We understood each other and when on the day of our last parting he said "Don't forget me" and I asked "Do you fear it" he said promptly "No," and needed no further answer.

---

1. Stow, Massachusetts was the ancestral home of John Randall.

I wish now I had written to him yet had no heart for trifles. What could I say save to utter and even repeat the exclamation "Do not get killed." I think no one knows him better than I and he felt that I knew him. I deemed him but half developed and mainly of slow growth though recently rapid.

There are many in the world doubtless as worthy to be loved but I never knew any one like him. How little is the rebel who killed him aware how precious a life he has extinguished. Full of penetration, his perception of character was intuitive; full of refined sensibility, he despised all meanness; social and full of genial humor he possessed the highest self-respect.

His confiding nature earnestly desired friendship but would have waited forever in loneliness rather than have wasted time or affection on the unworthy. He joined great force of will to the generosity and benevolence of his grandfather. He was somewhat obstinate which is natural to his age yet without force of will we are nothing.

His fine moral qualities would have saved him from excess and kept him well tempered to the last. . . . On our journey to the north I observed his fine taste in landscape and the activity and accuracy of all his senses. He had a fine ear for music and an eye for form which would have made him a skillful draughtsman. And he delighted in fine etchings.[2]

I would say no more now. To speak is to be choked, and to think is to be broken hearted, and tis better that I write than see you for I am in no condition to witness the emotions of another or to restrain my own. For many years I have watched this flower. At last, I saw it begin to bud and when just about to burst into blossom and fragrance, the tempest snaps its stalk and it withers away. . . .

With this peaceful sentiment will I close, ere the mind again passes that interval which separates the reactions of sorrow. . . . I have not restrained my emotions nor guarded my language from a fear to distress you for I know that

2. See page 77 for a discussion of Randall's collection of prints and etchings.

the best consolation where no consolation can be is the sympathy of a similar grief.

To Emily, sympathy and remembrance.

Your friend,
J. W. Randall

Winona, [Minnesota]
July 28th, 1863

Dear Mamma,

Stanley was to me like my own brother. I loved him very dearly. During the long visit I made in Beverly the winter before I went south, he and I came very near together, and I learned to love him deeply. I shall never forget the pleasant evenings we spent together in the old sitting room. He would sit by me and talk of his hopes and plans for the future and tell me all his thoughts and feelings. Wild boyish fancies often, yet underlying them all such an earnest seeking after truth and determination to live by it, such perfect detestation of all that was low and mean, of all that was done for mere show that I could not but feel that he would develop into a true man. I was often surprised at the depth and strength of his love for all home relations he was usually so reserved and undemonstrative. . . .

He is "safe" now and no more suffering will fall to his lot. It is hard to feel that I shall never see him again, but it is only for myself and those left behind that I can mourn. For him there is no need to grieve, he passed away while striving nobly for the right, and he must be happy now. It is at least a comfort to know that he died so quietly without much suffering.

My heart aches for you and Emmie and I would that I could help you, but you know where to look for strength and comfort better than I can tell you.

Ever your loving daughter,
Katie[3]

---

3. Wife of Francis Ellingwood Abbot.

Afterword

And glory long has made the sages smile;
'Tis something, nothing, words, illusion, wind—
Depending more upon the historian's style
Than on the name a person leaves behind.
                              —Lord Byron, *Don Juan*

Edwin writes about Stanley's last words:

His last words to me.
I found it in his valise, the only letter there.
Unfinished.

Camp Sykes Division
Near Henry House, Virginia
February 13, 1863

Dear Brother,
It seems as if I could understand just how lonely and
empty hearted you must feel sometimes for I too have
often felt lonely and empty hearted not because God had
taken my friends from me but because I had driven their
love away; but although my sorrow was not an inevitable
hungering yet it was very bitter and so I think I can
sympathize with yours. Indeed I have often thought that
I can feel your feelings perfectly almost, and frequently
when my words have been most harsh and cruel I have

[acted] with a double nature, one savage one in my own breast, another suffering one in yours.

The same feeling comes over me frequently now, I don't know, it seems as if I were you somehow. I can tell how you will feel and what you will say under given circumstances, almost as surely as I can in regard to myself. There is a wonderful brotherhood of nature as well as of blood between us I think. I think for certain that you perfectly understand what my words imperfectly express. And so I believe I feel how you drive away your transient [feelings] of despondency which you would be more than human if you could forever keep away from you.

When the lesson of submission has been so completely learned that regretful thoughts never steal into our hearts, why should we live longer? Is not our appointed work accomplished then? Yes, I think I believe that now. I think I understand that submission is the only real virtue. I have often puzzled my head to get it some unselfish motive for being good and how I am quite sure that I recognize as true what [life] taught you long ago.

I have not got to the point from which you started long years ago by the same road that led you hither. Mine has been longer and dustier and more perplexing. You were transported there by the perception of truth. I have groped thither though heaven only knows how much of darkness and doubt and skepticism almost. But I am quite certain that we are journeying now upon the same track—you hundreds of miles ahead and yet wonderfully near to me too. You are Great Heart I think, who have come back to show me the way.

You must not misunderstand me though. I do not think we will ever kneel at the same altar but, Edwin, do you think it matters much so we both worship the same God? After all, every mind has its peculiarity and no two can see everything absolutely out of one pair of eyes. It would be very pleasant to walk hand in hand with you through both the world of mind and of matter, but as inexorable necessity has apparently forbidden the one may it not also have forbidden the other? Nay, may it not be one of my temptations the

desire to bend a little what seems the truth to me in order
that our apparent [togetherness] may be greater?

Brief sketches below outline what happened after Stanley's death to those he left behind. It is important to note
that Stanley was not forgotten. His name lived on. During the
next ten years, four siblings and Uncle Harris each named a
child Stanley. To this day the descendants of Uncle Harris and
Brother Willie bear his name, as does the Philip Stanley Abbot
Pass above Lake Louise in the Canadian Rockies, named for
Edwin's son.

Edward Stanley Abbot (Stanley)

Stanley was laid to rest in the family plot in Central Cemetery of
Beverly, Massachusetts with his grandparents and great grandparents on a hill overlooking the sea—the same sea at which
he gazed with dreams of becoming a writer before entering Phillips Exeter Academy.

On the wall of Harvard Memorial Hall in Cambridge, Massachusetts, there stands today a permanent marble memorial
dating from 1874. Stanley's name leads the list of six classmates from the Class of 1864, all of whom died to preserve
the Union.

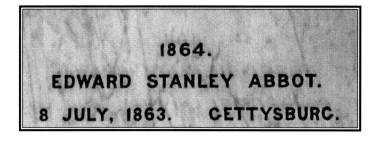

HARVARD MEMORIAL HALL PLAQUE

Several years before his death Stanley composed the following poem which might well serve as his epitaph.

My Epitaph
Blame not this child of frail humanity
That this old, crumbling tablet bears his name.
It was his last, poor harmless vanity
To make in death still one more bid for fame.

Joseph Hale Abbot (Hale)

While Stanley and his father did not have an especially good relationship, Hale expressed to Henry his strong feelings on the death of his son.

Beverly
October 9, 1863

Dear Henry,
    It would be useless to say I do not feel my new grief pressing heavily on my heart. I would not call your noble brother back—but here, where everything reminds me of all he endured in his struggle into manhood—which was often dull, harmful to his generous impulsive nature, I have truly shed more tears since my return, in remembering this, than the thought of his untimely death has caused to fall. It is a comfort to me to know that his last was his happiest year since boyhood. He would have made a noble man—why cannot I think only that he yet lives—lives where growth and happiness are eternal!
                                    Father

Hale retired from teaching at the Beverly High School in 1868. He died on April 7, 1873 in Cambridge where he was living with his daughter Emily.

Fanny Larcom Abbot (Fanny)

Stanley's death was a heavy blow to his mother. About two weeks after his death, she poured out her feelings in a letter to Henry.

> Cambridge
> July 23, 1863
>
> My dear Henry,
>
> How gladly would your mother have read you her whole heart if you could have the power of so doing bestowed upon you—yet how utterly impossible it is for her to write it to you, or even to tell it to you if you were here. . . . But what helps me to bear my heavy burden, how the all wise Father has been preparing me by his kind providence to meet this stunning blow, is what will more interest and console you now with regard to me. . . .
>
> Yesterday in the clear light of one of the loveliest of summer days, in that sacred spot which he loved, where our other precious ones repose, I gave back "ashes to ashes—dust to dust." My brave beautiful boy—oh how willing would I have lain down in his stead! I know his spirit has returned to God who gave it. He was good and true—and I ought to be glad for him that he has been permitted thus early to escape the windy storm and tempest of our present life—but He does not forbid my yearning heart to grieve that I shall see that beloved form no more in earth—no more to meet his warm embrace—hear his bounding step—his cheerful voice.
>
> Your own loving Mother

In 1869, Fanny moved in with Henry after Willie left home for college and the Beverly house inherited from her father was sold. Fanny died on June 26, 1883 in Cambridge, Massachusetts.

Henry Larcom Abbot (Henry)

Henry had a distinguished career in the Army Engineers, both during and after the Civil War, attaining the rank of Brigadier General and Commander of the Army Engineer Corps. Among his chief accomplishments were a classic study of the flow and control of the Mississippi River and recommendations to Congress for the location and design of the Panama Canal. He retired to Cambridge, Massachusetts and died there on October, 21 1927.

Henry's daughter, born six months after Stanley's death, bore the name, Marion Stanley Abbot.

A book by Catherine Abbot, the wife of Henry's great grand-son, provides a substantial account of his life and role in the family.[1]

Edwin Hale Abbot (Edwin or Eddie) and Martha Trask Steele (Mattie)

Edwin practiced law in Boston until 1876. For many years he was closely identified with the Harriman, Gould, and Vander-bilt railroad interests. In 1873, he became general solicitor and a director of the Wisconsin Central Railway Company. He moved to Milwaukee in 1876, and subsequently became the railway's president, in which role he served until 1890. He was also a director of the Northern Pacific Railway. In 1889 he returned to Cambridge, building a mansion with its own elec-tric generator before electricity was commercially available. The mansion is now the site of the Longy School of Music.

Stanley's letters to Cousin Mattie were with Edwin's Family Papers at Yale. The reason was obvious once I connected the dots. Toward the end of my research, I discovered Mattie's last

---

1. Abbot, *Family Letters of General Henry Larcom Abbot*, 45.

name and recognized it. Suddenly I understood! On the day of Stanley's reburial in Central Cemetery, Beverly, Massachusetts, Edwin wrote to Mattie.

> Boston, Massachusetts
> July 23, 1863
>
> My dear Cousin [Mattie],
>
> I have brought his body home and today we lay it where the dust of his kindred rest, in Beverly. . . . Among the few papers and letters in his haversack I found the enclosed letter to you.[2] It was apparently finished and waiting for a mail. It bears the same date with the last letter I received from him. It is probably the last letter he ever wrote. I now send it to you. . . . I know you were a very dear friend and all who were his friends are mine. Someday perhaps we may ourselves become better acquainted. Meantime we have a past in common.
>
> Sincerely, your friend,
> Edwin H. Abbot

Edwin and Mattie did become better acquainted and developed a future in common. Three years later, on September 19, 1866, Martha Trask Steele married Edwin Hale Abbot in Portland, Maine. Edwin and Mattie had two sons. Their firstborn was Philip Stanley Abbot whose middle name was the one both had known so well. Philip died from a mountain-climbing accident above Lake Louise in the Canadian Rockies. His death led to the development of a system of mountain guides throughout the region. To this day, above Lake Louise lies the Abbot Pass Refuge Cabin, National Historic Site of Canada, yet another tribute to Stanley's memory, albeit indirectly.

Edwin continued to be true to his caring, nurturing nature, as amply demonstrated in his relationship with Stanley, and later exemplified by his adoption of Gladys Elizabeth Pearson, an orphan girl, at the request of Fanny, who had been a friend

---

2. See letter to Mattie from Stanley dated June 28, 1863 on page 209.

of Gladys's grandfather.[3] Gladys was later known as Constance Abbot.

The desire to control others also persisted as one of Edwin's notable traits. According to family lore, Edwin paid the Harvard tuition for one of his nephews who, like Stanley, did not devote as much attention to his studies as Edwin wished. Hence, Edwin refused to finance the college education of another nephew.

Edwin died on May 30, 1927 and Mattie on December 20, 1932 in Cambridge, Massachusetts.

Francis Ellingwood Abbot (Frank)

Frank became a noted philosopher, theologian, editor, teacher, and author. As a leader of the "Free Church" movement, he sought to reconstruct theology in accordance with Darwin's scientific method.

Frank's son born on December 13, 1863, five months after Stanley's death, was named Edward Stanley Abbot. The second Edward Stanley Abbot had a distinguished career as a psychiatrist associated with the McLean Hospital, a psychiatric institution in Belmont, Massachusetts.

A Harvard University archivist captured the "love eternal" of Frank and his wife Katie in a compilation of his diary and their letters.[4] Frank committed suicide at the grave of his beloved Katie on October 23, 1903, the tenth anniversary of her death.

William Fitzhale Abbot (Willie)

Willie became a teacher like his father. Following his graduation from Harvard, Willie taught for several years at a private

---

3. William F. Abbot's handwritten note in his copy of *Descendants of George Abbott of Rowley* by Lemuel Abbott.
4. Francis Ellingwood Abbot, *If Ever Two Were One: A Diary of Love Eternal*, ed. Brian A. Sullivan (New York: Regan Books, 2004).

school in Indianapolis, Indiana. Finally, he settled in Worcester, Massachusetts where he taught at Classical High School for over forty years.

Willie was the family genealogist of his generation, retaining letters and other records, while producing both published and unpublished summaries of the family history. Stanley's name lived on in Willie's grandson, Hale Stanley Abbot, and continues in a great grandson, Stanley Hale Abbot. Willie died on April 21, 1922, before the death of his two oldest brothers.

Emily Frances Abbot (Emmie)

Emmie married a distant cousin, Abiel Abbot Vaughan. Their son who was born in 1870 was named Stanley Vaughan. She was active in church work and an amateur watercolor artist. She died on November 5, 1899.

Harris and Caroline Ann Butler Abbot (Harris and Annie)

Harris and Annie lived out their lives farming the Abbot Homestead in Wilton, New Hampshire. They named their first child, born on October 20, 1863—three months after Stanley's death—Stanley Harris Abbot after the nephew who had stayed four months with them prior to pursuing a military career. The name lives on in Harris's great grandson, Stanley James Abbot.

Abbot Homestead

Stanley Harris Abbot inherited the Abbot Homestead in Wilton, New Hampshire from his father, and he continued to farm the land. When Stanley's son Howard Abbot died in a farm accident in 1936, his brother Charles Mack Abbot inherited the farm. It was sold out of the family after the Second World War when property taxes on farmland became too great to make farming a profitable occupation. The house survives, but no member of the Abbot family resides there today.

Bibliography

Abbot, Catherine C. *Family Letters of General Henry Larcom Abbot, 1831–1927*. Gettysburg: Thomas Publications, 2001.

Abbot, Charles G. *Uncles*. Washington: Self-published, 1949.

Abbot, Edwin H. "Edward Stanley Abbot." In *Harvard Memorial Biographies*, edited by Thomas Higginson, vol. II, 425–435. Cambridge: Sever and Francis, 1866.

Abbot, Fanny Larcom. "My Father's Shipwreck." In *Atlantic Monthly*, August 1871, 144–160.

Abbot, Francis Ellingwood. *If Ever Two Were One: A Private Diary of Love Eternal*. Edited by Brian A. Sullivan. New York: Regan Books, 2004.

Abbott, Maj. Lemuel Abijah. *Descendants of George Abbott of Rowley, Massachusetts*. Boston: Self-published, 1906.

Abbot, William F. "Genealogy of the Larcom Family." In *The Essex Institute Historical Collections*, vol. 58, nos. 1 and 2 (1922), 41–48, 129–150.

————. *Joseph Hale Abbot: A Memorial Tribute by his Youngest Son*. Boston: Self-published, 1890.

Adams, Hannah. *A Summary History of New England*. Dedham: Self-published, 1799.

Blackmar, Frank W, ed. *Kansas: A Cyclopedia of State History*, vol. II. Chicago: Standard Publishing Company, 1912.

Coco, Gregory A. *A Strange and Blighted Land, Gettysburg: The Aftermath of a Battle*. Gettysburg: Thomas Publications, 1996.

Ellis, William Arba, comp. and ed. *Norwich University, 1819–1911: Her History, Her Graduates, Her Roll of Honor,* vol. 2. Montpelier: Major-General Grenville M. Dodge, 1911.

Goodheart, Adam, "The Shrug That Made History." *New York Times Magazine,* April 3, 2011.

Goodwin, Doris Kearns. *Team of Rivals: The Political Genius of Abraham Lincoln.* New York: Simon and Schuster, 2005.

Hardee, Lieut.-Col. W. J. *Rifle and Light Infantry Tactics for the Exercise and Manœuvres of Troops When Acting as Light Infantry or Riflemen.* Prepared under the Direction of the War Department. Philadelphia: Lippincott, Grambo & Co., 1855.

LaFantasie, Glenn W. *Twilight at Little Round Top: July 2, 1863—The Tide Turns at Gettysburg.* New York: John Wiley & Sons, Inc., 2005.

Livermore, Abiel Abbot and Sewall Putnam. *History of the Town of Wilton, Hillsborough County, New Hampshire.* Lowell: Marden & Rowell, 1888.

Moore, Frank. *Diary of the American Revolution: From Newspapers and Original Documents,* vol. II. New York: Charles Scribner, 1860.

Pfanz, Harry W. *Gettysburg: The Second Day.* Chapel Hill: The University of North Carolina Press, 1987.

Project Gutenberg eBook of *Cato,* 2010.

Randall, John Witt. *Poems of Nature and Life.* Boston: George H. Ellis, 1899.

Reese, Timothy J. *Sykes' Regular Infantry Division, 1861–1864: A History of Regular United States Infantry Operations in the Civil War's Eastern Theater.* Jefferson, North Carolina: McFarland & Company, 1990.

Robinson, Solon, and N. Orr, illus. *Hot Corn: Life Scenes in New York Illustrated, including, the Story of Little Katy, Madalina, the Rag-Picker's Daughter, Wild Maggie, etc.* New York: De Witt and Davenport, 1854.

Russell, J. Almus, "Found: Site of the First Starch Mill." In
    Yankee, October 1969.

Sears, Stephen W. *Gettysburg*. Boston: Houghton Mifflin Com-
    pany, 2003.

Seymour, George Dudley. *Captain Nathan Hale, Major John
    Palsgrave Wyllys: A Digressive History*. New Haven:
    Self-published, 1933.

*War of the Rebellion: A Compilation of the Official Records
    of the Union and Confederate Armies*, vol. XXVII.
        Washington, D.C.: Government Printing Office, 1880.

Ward, Geoffrey G. with Ric Burns and Ken Burns. *The Civil
    War: An Illustrated History*. New York: Alfred A.
    Knopf, Inc., 1990.

Woodbury, Charles. "Independence Park, Beverly, Massachu-
    setts." Joint Standing Committee on Printing.
    Beverly, Massachusetts, 1906.

ARCHIVES

Abbot Archives, West Hartford, Connecticut. In the author's possession. Contains: (1) Correspondence between Stanley and Mother, Father, Sister Emily, Cousin Emily, and Brother Willie; (2) Stanley's journal from February, 1860 to April, 1860; (3) Excerpts by Sister Emily from Stanley's journal from September, 1860 to May, 1863; (4) Various school and other documents including a notebook of Stanley's poems, a copybook containing Stanley's excerpts from writings by others; and (5) A folder of drawings by Stanley.

Edwin Hale Abbot Family Papers, Manuscripts and Archives, Yale University Library, New Haven, Connecticut. Contains: (1) Correspondence between Stanley and Brother Edwin; (2) Correspondence between Stanley and Cousin Mattie; (3) Letters from Henry to Edwin; (4) Support Agreement for Stanley by Edwin and Henry; (5) Stanley's Will; (6) Support Agreement for Fanny and children by Edwin and Henry; (7) Letters and other documents concerning Stanley's Army performance at Gettysburg and before.

Francis Ellingwood Abbot Family Papers, Manuscripts and Archives, Andover-Harvard Theological Library, Harvard Divinity School, Cambridge, Massachusetts. Contains correspondence between Stanley and Frank.

Henry L. Abbot Family Papers, Library of Congress, Washington, District of Columbia. Correspondence, memoirs, diaries, writings, photographs, legal and financial records, genealogical material, military records, printed matter, and mementos.

INDEX

Page numbers in *italics* indicate illustrations.

235

About the Author

Quincy Abbot inherited from his grandfather William Fitzhale Abbot an interest in the family history, along with an accumulation of family papers and other artifacts dating back to the late 1700's. He is a graduate of Williams College, a Fellow of the Society of Actuaries, and an elected Member of the American Antiquarian Society.

He is the father of four daughters. Since the birth of his second daughter with intellectual disabilities, Mr. Abbot has been an advocate for individuals with disabilities. He was President of The Arc United States.

Mr. Abbot is the recipient of many awards including the Connecticut AARP Andrus Award for Community Service, the Wyoming Seminary Distinguished Service Award, the Connecticut Spirit of the ADA Award, and the Lifetime Achievement Award of the National Conference of Executives of The Arc United States.

Quincy Abbot retired in 1990 from CIGNA as Senior Vice President in charge of its tax operations throughout the world, and he currently resides in West Hartford, Connecticut.

JUST

a Little

More

TIME

56 Authors
on Love and Loss

Reprints

"Wake-up Call" and "Dear Dad" were originally printed in *Unexpected Strength,* Copyright © 2016 by Weber School District.

"The Gifts of a Teacher" was first published in *The Wall Street Journal.*

"Walking Distance" originally appeared in *Subject to Change: True Stories from the Temescal Memoir Writers,* a limited edition anthology of the Community Memoir Project, directed by Frances Lefkowitz and funded by Cal Humanities, a nonprofit partner of the National Endowment for the Humanities (Paper in my Shoe Press, 2015).

"Waking Up" was printed in *Through Our Eyes: In Black and White,* Copyright © 2015 by Weber School District.

A different version of "Airport Gifts" was originally published as "What's Your Problem, Mom?" in *When One Door Closes: Reflections from Women on Life's Turning Points.*

"Alone" was first published in the 2010–2011 *San Diego Poetry Annual.*

A different version of "Breaking My Silence" was originally printed in *Tarnished* (Pinchback Press).

ISBN 978-0-9985257-1-6